LONDON TRANSPORT

BUSES & COACHES

1962

LONDON TRANSPORT
BUSES & COACHES

1962

John A.S. Hambley

Published in 1998 by
JOHN A.S. HAMBLEY
7 Linden Road,
Dunstable,
Beds. LU5 4NZ

Additional text and research by David A. Ruddom

British Library Cataloguing in Publication Data
A catalogue record for this book is available from the British Library

ISBN 0 9533146 0 X

Front cover photograph:
Having just left the busy Golders Green station forecourt, RT241 sets out on its rather circuitous journey to Southgate Station. This bus had first entered service in December 1947 operating out of Croydon garage and after use at Thornton Heath reached its present home of Muswell Hill in December 1958. This was to be its last operational base as in February 1963 it was delicensed and moved to Edmonton garage to await disposal which came in the November. (Alan Mortimer)

Back cover photograph:
A normal resident of Leyton garage, RF438 is seen at Clapton Pond on 11th April while on loan to Dalston. Although the 208 route required more buses at weekends and loans for this purpose at that time were not uncommon, this is a Wednesday and perhaps Dalston were suffering from a shortage of serviceable buses. Very conveniently the duty number plate 10 has been slotted over the painted garage code T. (John Gascoine)

Designed by Hedgehog and produced by Hughes & Company, Kempsey, Worcestershire.
Printed and bound in Great Britain.

Protruding from the doorway of Amersham garage are GS28, overhauled in September 1961 and GS56 which received similar treatment in January 1963, which was not before time considering its dowdy appearance and lack of paint on the roof. It has worked into the garage from Route 348 but with the common practice of interworking between routes within the Country Area it will probably find itself in service on another route next time it ventures out. Amersham had been involved with this type of bus for passenger service since December 1953 but they had all left by 24th October of the year under review having been replaced by OMO RF class buses. (Alan Mortimer)

Acknowledgements

This series of books continues to give me immense pleasure during the number of hours that have been spent in selecting images from a wealth of material for inclusion within the pages of this 1962 volume. David Ruddom I know feels the same and he must be singled out for a special thank you for his continuing support and enthusiasm in editing the captions which hopefully bring the pictures to life. John G.S.Smith has contributed on numerous occasions with recollections and comments and his help has proved invaluable. Enthusiasts and historians of the London bus and coach scene continue to correspond and invariably allow me to use their photographic work in this series and in that respect I must thank the following for their help in this particular volume:

Dave Berwick, Bespix (Brian Speller), Alan B Cross, A.J.Douglas, John Gascoine, L.G.Hooley, Fred W.Ivey, D.A.Jones, Kevin Lane, Mrs.B.Legg, Roy Marshall, G.R.Mills, Alan Mortimer, Tony R.Packer, Douglas F.Parker, Roger Partridge, Michael Rooum, Tom Smith, Ray Stanmore, Ralph E.Stevens, J.C.Walker and Ron Wellings.

All through the many long sessions of the selection process and discussions our ladies, my wife Iris and David's wife Enid, have fed, watered and tolerated our particular interest in road transport and a big thank you must be voiced here to them both. The factual information on which the captions are based has come from an increasing number of individuals and published sources. Grateful acknowledgement is hereby made to everyone concerned and to the London Historical Research Group of the Omnibus Society, the London Omnibus Traction Society, the PSV Circle and the RT/RF Register for continued reference to their many publications.

Publishers Note

Comment has been made in certain quarters regarding the non-appearance of books for the years 1957, 1958, 1959 and 1960. I can assure you that work on all of them is in progress and the sole reason for them having been by-passed at present is a shortage of suitable prints currently held on file to eventually form the basis of the individual titles. It would seem that London bus photographers got bored in these years and stopped carrying their cameras!

I would therefore ask that if you have a collection of prints which you feel might be appropriate for this series of books and in particular these years, please get in touch with me at the address shown earlier. If the negative of a particular print has been mislaid over the years, Kevin Lane can make a new one as well as providing a service for the developing and printing of black and white postcard prints. He can be reached at 15 Beech Green, Dunstable, LU6 1EB or by telephone on 01582 601458. Alternatively I would certainly pass on any messages. A further service he provides is the production of black and white prints from colour transparencies which in turn could be used in future books.

The listings associated with this series of books are once again available. The fleet number (7th edition) lists all vehicles shown in the books up to and including the thirteen in the series to be published. The route number edition (6th) is correct up to and including the eleventh book. They are only available direct from the author at Dunstable and are priced at £5.00 each including post and packing. Information given includes fleet number, registration number, route or service engaged on, location, source of photograph with year and page number of the book in which it is published. It only remains for me to add that I sincerely hope you enjoy the selection of prints used in this book of a most interesting period in the history of London Transport.

Introduction

1962 will be remembered for the end of the use of electric traction on road passenger services in London, at least until the Croydon Tramlink, currently under construction, is completed. After 8th May diesel powered buses and coaches reigned supreme. Electric tram services had begun on a regular basis in April 1901 between Shepherds Bush or Hammersmith and Kew Bridge, although a tramway within the Alexandra Palace grounds had operated with electricity in 1898. Trolleybus services had commenced in May 1931 and road services were partly operated with electric power for sixty one years.

Concurrently with the trolleybus conversion programme, which had commenced in 1959, the RM class of bus was being delivered as the replacement and these were first used in this way in stage 4 which took place on 11th November 1959. Once the programme was complete attention could focus on replacing the post-war RT family of buses, although this was not without its problems.

The intention was to replace the 56 seat RTs initially on outer routes with 64 seat RMs on a nine buses for ten basis. This was one of several sticking points at the time between Unions and Management, others being the proposal to expand the RML fleet and also to introduce high capacity standee buses in Central London. After seven months of stalemate plans to introduce Routemasters at Harrow Weald and Edgware were abandoned and instead replacement of RTs began in December on a one to one basis at Tottenham, Mortlake, Stockwell and Putney on routes 73 and 37 followed within a few days by Hendon and Rye Lane on route 13. Tottenham's allocation was also used for the night route N90 and at weekends the new buses appeared on other routes from these garages. The final garage to receive RMs at the end of the year was Cricklewood who began the conversion of the busy 16 route. All the Stockwell and Mortlake allocation and most of Tottenham's were Leyland engined and at first the throaty roar they produced seemed odd in what up to then had been an AEC vehicle.

The new Routemaster Green Line coaches (RMC class) did however enter service in the late summer and autumn and although all were delivered in 1962 later members did not start work until the following year. The unique forward entrance RMF1254 appeared at the Commercial Motor Exhibition held in October with blinds for route 104, although this proved to be of no significance despite contemporary rumour. Other new deliveries included the AEC Regent V, registered 220CXK, for the B.E.A. fleet and the AEC Renown registered 8071ML, which later received the fleet number RX1, was taken on loan to enter service at Northfleet in February of the following year.

The influx of new vehicle deliveries consisted of RML902/3; RM1072/5 - 1253/5 - 1383/5/6 and RMF1254 which together with 220CKX and 8071ML made a total of 383 new vehicles.

The remnants of two classes of buses ran in service for the last time during the year. T787 was withdrawn from service at Crawley in August having been used latterly on routes 426 and 852 while TD124 was the last of the class to operate on route 240A in October. Sales amounted to just eight 2RT2s with six of the post war variety also departing. Three RTLs with eleven members of the TD class made up a total of 28 vehicles, a small number compared to what was to happen in the following years although to offset this the residue of the trolleybus fleet went in 1962.

A test of overhaul procedures was carried out at Aldenham on RM36 during February prior to two further members being attended to although full scale overhaul of the class did not materialise until the following year. While this was taking place RTW255 emerged from the works in April with the distinction of being the very last of its class to receive an overhaul.

As far as trips to foreign places go RM546 followed up its two excursions of the previous year with a journey to Stockholm in May for use in conjunction with a British Trade Fair. RM1272 visited Geneva during September and October while RML898 made the long journey to San Francisco for a 'London Week' during November.

As with the previous few years there was much activity with the bus service network. New routes included the 5B, 29B, 33, 135A, 230A, 249B, 292 and in the Country Area the 372 which only lasted a few months. Direct trolleybus replacement routes were 245, 260, 266, 267, 281, 282, 283, 285 and 293. Many alterations in the form of extensions, revisions and sectionalisation of routes were brought into operation, some again in connection with trolleybus replacement. In the Country Area several Sunday services disappeared, symptomatic of the future, and the 366 and 397 numbers dropped out of use for the time being.

Other notable highlights of the year were the closure of West Green garage, the old 'Admiral' base, on 3rd January while work on the new Hatfield garage commenced during March although it was not to open until May 1963.

Standing within Onslow Street bus station, Guildford awaiting their respective departure times two very different bodied AEC Regent Mk III chassis. RT4727 on the left with high bridge bodywork by Weymann carries an unusual information blind for its use on route 408A. On the right of the picture RLH13 carries another Weymann body this time a low bridge example which seats three passengers less than the RT. Wheel arch assemblies are also completely different as is the shape and height of the radiators. (Douglas F. Parker)

The Sunday service on Route 88 had received an extension beyond Belmont Station to Banstead Hospital in 1961 and this far flung destination looks a little out of place with the background of Selfridges and the Oxford Street shops. Stockwell's RTL1301 passes the window shoppers on its lengthy journey. (Ron Wellings)

At the eastern terminus of Route 153, a Sunday only operation, RT4258 emerges from Plumstead garage for its long haul to West Hampstead. Now showing wear this Park Royal bodied bus had originally entered service carrying a Saunders built example. Unfortunately due to this body exchange that took place in August 1958 an early exit from its London haunts to pastures further afield with the Ayrshire Bus Owners Association was assured. The sticker fixed to the rearmost lower deck window announces that work is available for drivers and conductors while the telephone number on the front advertisements reminds us that it was not until March 1966 that all figure numbers were introduced. (Alan Mortimer)

The high point of a ride on Route 233 was the view from the road below the terrace of Alexandra Palace although close examination of this picture reveals a lot of activity among the passengers of the bus, some of whom are more interested in the photographer. The 'Children' road sign on the lamppost emphasises the recreational nature of the area. The bus is RT1238, one of those transferred over to Wood Green in January from West Ham at the time West Green garage closed and the pleasant summer's day is 24th June. (John Gascoine)

Craven bodied RT1480, entered service in September 1949 from Potters Bar garage and was disposed of in April 1956. Now this ex-Londoner looks immaculate in the colour scheme of the Garelochhead Coach Services Ltd. This was the third bus and coach operator of this vehicle since initial sale by the Executive and nearly as many years were spent by the bus in service outside London as was served within the capital. It is seen at Garelochhead, which despite the title was quite a considerable distance from the owner's registered address in Dumbarton. (Alan Mortimer)

RW2 crosses the bridge over the railway at Elstree & Borehamwood Station with a leafless background sometime during January. The style of anti-climb fence with diagonal slats was very much a Midland Railway feature. The bus has come from the terminus at Cowley Hill on the northern fringes of Borehamwood and is now heading up Allum Lane on its journey to Harpenden. At this time all 355s ran this way rather than the later routeing through Theobald Street to Radlett. Note the use of lower case lettering for the intermediate points served on the new blinds provided for the move of these vehicles to St.Albans. (Ron Wellings)

Seen at the top of Brixton Hill RT4238, with Saunders bodywork, works duty BN7 as it journeys to Tooting Broadway. Weekday Route 95 still follows the roads served by Tram Service 10 which it had replaced eleven years earlier. Last overhauled in February, the RT's previous sphere of operation had been Croydon followed by Norwood garages, confirming its attachment to the southern area of Central bus operation. (Alan Mortimer)

The background to RT643 is typical of the architecture of the boom years in the development of the new towns. The bus dates from September 1948 when it entered service at Grays garage carrying Weymann built RT3 body number 1892. Prior to the date of its disposal in May 1964 it had received this Park Royal built RT10 body numbered 2267. The RT10 classification indicated its capability of being mounted on either an RT or RTL chassis. Here it works the 805 route in First Avenue, Harlow heading out west to Little Parndon. (Alan B.Cross)

The normally seething Camden High Street is almost deserted as Tottenham's RF451 goes about its early morning duties collecting and transporting London Transport Underground staff to their places of work. A Ford Consul car shares the road with the RF and it is obvious that the photographer is regarded as a strange curiosity at this ungodly hour. (Alan Mortimer)

The lady passenger in the front seat behind the cab looks particularly frustrated at the wait caused by the crew change opposite the Pound at Sutton. The Sutton shopping centre is not that far away but passengers must wait for the new crew to appear who will take RT307 on to Belmont Station. Early in the following year this fleet number could not be seen in the capital as the bus left for pastures new around Tewkesbury, being acquired by Warner Motors.
(Alan Mortimer)

On Saturdays Route 18 used an allocation of RTW type buses spare from their Monday to Friday use on other routes operated by Willesden garage. Here, as RTW8 passes Stonebridge Park garage on its way to the 'Swan' at Sudbury, one can almost hear the familiar rasp produced from its Leyland 9.8 litre engine. The trolleybus wires have been removed but the extraction team have still to remove the standards including A240. RTW8 upon its sale by the Board in December 1966 joined many of its sisters in Ceylon. (Alan Mortimer)

RM1143 first entered passenger service in May of the year under review and on 7th September is seen parked at its home garage of Hounslow awaiting its call to duty. These new vehicles replaced RTs previously used on the route prior to the last stage of the trolleybus conversion programme which took place on 9th May. Route 117 was then extended over the roads hitherto served by trolleybuses on Route 657, hence its claim to the new vehicles. (Tom Smith)

The GS class of bus only commenced operation at Grays garage in the year under review when new route 372 was introduced on 18th June to run a local service within the Belhus Estate. GS34 is seen in service on a positioning journey on Route 328 after operating the new route. This was the only small capacity bus then used in passenger service at Grays and was to be transferred to Hertford upon the failure of the 372 service on 23rd October. The garage were once again not involved with the class until in June 1965 another new route, 399 running through the Dartford Tunnel, required the use of a GS. (Ron Wellings)

Seen standing in New Cross Road opposite NX garage, Rye Lane garage's RT3327 operates on Route 36B to Grove Park. This bus had seen service at Palmers Green and Edgware before arriving at its present and last operating base, being withdrawn from service in June 1964 and disposed of in September. The chassis dates from 1951 while the body is a little older being manufactured in 1948 when it first appeared mounted on the chassis of RT569. In its post London career RT3327 was operated by the Ceylon Transport Board receiving local registration number 23-SRI-1238. (Alan Mortimer)

Bus route 207, once trolleybus 607, and remaining trolleybus service 657 share the same stand at Shepherds Bush before their separate departures to Uxbridge, as displayed by RT2979 and to Hounslow in the case of the trolleybuses. RMs were the more normal allocation to the 207 but in 1962 Uxbridge garage provided five RTs on Sundays to support the Hanwell Routemasters. (Tony R.Packer)

Route 164A shared Morden Underground Station as a terminal with Route 164 and followed the same roads to the cross roads at Banstead. The 164 continued down Fir Tree Road while the 164A variant turned left along the arterial road until at Tattenham Way it turned right to journey on to Tattenham Corner Station. In this picture RT388 has worked back from the southern terminus to Sutton Garage and has turned into Bushey Road at the erstwhile trolleybus terminus, its home base standing at right angles at the end of this short thoroughfare. (Alan Mortimer)

RT3156 had reached Luton garage for operation during January of the year under review and was to stay until the summer of 1965. With a background much changed over the years the RT is seen in Park Street, Luton on 28th April waiting for yet another run up Farley Hill to the village of Caddington on Route 360. The duty number LS8 is part of a sequence including Route 321 and does not imply that eight vehicles were needed on this short route. The bus currently carries Park Royal body number 3617, first carried by RT1655, having relinquished its original Weymann example upon its first overhaul. (Tony R.Packer)

GS84 looks very different from the condition it can be seen in on page 105 of the 1956 book of this series. Resting at the bus station in Crawley, situated on what was then part of Three Bridges Road and is now totally unrecognisable, it carries duty plates CY24 for its use on Route 852 to Horsham via Faygate. In May of the following year it was delicensed and placed in store to await sale in March 1964 to Tillingbourne Valley Services Ltd. of Chilworth. It moved into the preservation movement in 1970. (Alan Mortimer)

In the previous year RM632 had had the notability of being the first production RM to be fitted with a Leyland engine in place of the AEC unit it had when delivered new to London Transport in January. Midway through that month it left for an extended period, firstly at Self Changing Gears in Coventry before moving on to Leyland Motors Ltd. Arriving back in London in June with its new power unit it entered service operating from Hanwell garage later in the month. Seen here in 1962 traversing the Uxbridge Road and doubtless emitting its distinctive throaty roar, it heads for Uxbridge, the outer terminus of Route 207. (Alan Mortimer)

The long established 131 route between Hersham (Sundays), Walton on Thames and Kingston was utilised in the 14th stage of the trolleybus conversion programme to replace trolleybus 604. The route was extended beyond Kingston to Wimbledon and Norbiton garage received new RMs with which to operate it aided by a weekend injection of RTs from Merton. RM1209 is seen at West Molesey en-route to Wimbledon. (Alan Mortimer)

Early on in its ownership by J.Laurie and Co. of Hamilton ex-RTL12 was re-registered from its original JXN324 to YVA776. Ministry of Transport officials had found that registration documentation papers did not agree with the information found on the vehicle's chassis necessitating this unusual occurrence. The bus had first entered service with London Transport from West Green garage in December 1948 and received two overhauls before being disposed of in September 1958. The body shown is the original Park Royal example numbered 2225 which RTL12 had carried from new, albeit showing some cosmetic alterations. Although carrying Chieftain livery and fleet name the vehicle is actually owned by Central SMT and carries their fleet number HL190. (Alan Mortimer)

RF530 and RM227 are seen on 6th May while resting from their temporary training duties at Fulwell garage, although why the RF should be displaying the garage run in blind for Route 216 is a mystery. Since its return from its February overhaul it was to spend its next six months at the hands of new recruits, firstly from Norbiton and later Hounslow before entering service from Kingston in September. The RM on the other hand, new in February 1960, first entered service at Walthamstow two months later. In January of the year under review it was taken out of service and was to spend the intervening period until its first overhaul in July 1964 as a mechanical trainer visiting no fewer than a dozen different garages before re-entering service at its original garage. (John Gascoine)

In the depths of winter Barking's RT2808 works off route as it runs into the garage from its labours on Route 148. Parked cars including a rather new looking Ford Popular hinder the progress of the bus whose crew probably want no hold up to spoil their intending rest period. In December 1964 a journey to Cape Town ensured further passenger use for this RT with the Cape Electric Tramways system. (Alan Mortimer)

RT3868, garaged at Catford, operates on Sunday only Route 124A and is seen as it journeys to Eltham, Southend Crescent. This route number had been introduced with the summer programme of route changes on 11th May 1960 to differentiate the Sunday extension to Bexley Hospital from the 124 which now had journeys to Falconwood Parade. This particular RT had commenced work in September 1950 in Country Area livery from Swanley Junction garage. Upon its second overhaul in February 1959 it was outshopped in Central Area colours. (Ron Wellings)

RT4228 pulls away from the Marble Arch bus stop, its offside trafficator shining brightly in the rainy gloom. The weekday route 16 was operated in two sections - Victoria to Neasden and Kilburn Park to Sudbury Town but at weekends the service was operated as a through route. The bus had received an overhaul in August but the winter weather conditions have caused road grime to hide its bright paintwork. (Ron Wellings)

Newly delivered RM class buses appeared on the Sightseeing Bus Tour during May being operated from New Cross garage. The special advertising material carried by the six vehicles involved makes for interesting reading. The buses left every hour from Victoria, Buckingham Palace Road, the twenty mile tour taking two hours and for this adults paid 4/- (20p) while children went for 2/- (10p). The buses concerned were RMs 1168, 1169, 1177, 1178, 1195 and 1196 of which the highest numbered is seen with very few seats still to fill at the starting point of the tour on a sunny August day. (Tony R.Packer)

RF637 seems to be collecting a good load of passengers on its journey on Route 422 from Leatherhead to Boxhill, Greenacres. Although the blind quotes Headley and Pebblecombe as served by the route a check on the map shows that oddly it missed what might be termed the centre of both places. (Ron Wellings)

Ex-RTL149 is seen at the Royal Wells bus station, Cheltenham on 26th May. Its new owners were A.H.Kearsey in whose fleet it was numbered 69. They will be remembered by the picture of LT1202 which appeared in the 1956 book of this series appearing still to favour the same basic paint scheme with a little less of the relief colour. (Tony R.Packer)

The lower deck portion of the Dodson open topped, rear platform body once carried on the chassis of a 1925 built Dennis 4ton chassis peacefully deteriorates in the countryside at Battisford in Suffolk. The bus had originally been operated by the Gordon Omnibus Company Ltd. of Leyton before the fleet was acquired by the newly formed LPTB on 15th December 1933. Initially given fleet number D191 this was changed to D186 before the bus was withdrawn from service during 1934. After sale the chassis was used as the basis for a lorry which could still be seen in use in the post-war period while the body became the decrepit store seen here on 20th April, some twenty eight years later. (G.R.Mills)

RT79 traverses Chiswick High Road at Turnham Green on 1st May having now reached its twenty second year of working within the capital. It was May 1940 that this combination of AEC Regent chassis and LPTB built body (number 352) first entered service from Chelverton Road, Putney garage as a 2RT2. Eventually with modifications made in the area of the dynamo and reciprocating compressor the bus, along with a substantial number of its contemporaries, received the engineering code 3/2RT2/2. It was in May 1955 that Country Area livery was applied and transfer to its new operating territory in and around Hertford took place together with six of its sisters. Since its return to non-passenger duties it first saw use as a staff bus from Reigate garage and finally as a learner vehicle based at Dunton Green, eventually being disposed of in June 1963. (Bespix)

RT659 appears to have been left to deteriorate, having been earmarked for early disposal which took place in March of the following year. Leaning over from its sharp right hand turn out of Fanshawe Avenue into Longbridge Road at Barking, it nears the end of its journey from Barkingside on Route 169 which appropriately enough was the replacement in 1959 for trolleybus 691. Initially passing to H & C Transport of Garston it was only a few months before this AEC Regent Mark III with Park Royal bodywork moved on to spend many years with J.Lloyd & Sons of Nuneaton. (Alan Mortimer)

Waiting for use on Route 240A on 1st May at Edgware are TD121 and TD104 with an inspector and clippie making use of the front wheel arch to have a conversation. The bus nearest to the camera working duty EW5 will complete the full route to Mill Hill East Station while the other on duty EW1 will work only as far as the Broadway. Neither bus was exported after sale by LTE, as was the case with so many of the class but they went their separate ways for use as non p.s.v. with different owners. TD121 was eventually acquired for preservation in 1966 but as a result of vandalism had to be dismantled in 1968. (Tom Smith)

With autumn fast appoaching in this picture of RT1091, a goodly number of passengers are waiting at Slough to board the bus for Windsor Castle. In December 1965 this RT would visit Aldenham for overhaul and re-emerge in Central bus colours. Here however it is still working in the Country Area it has served since 1949. Of interest is the rather odd slipboard carried on the bulkhead which announces in no uncertain terms that the bus is working on Route 441A despite the canopy blind saying otherwise. This was probably wise since the 441A was an early nineteen sixties oddity which provided the Sunday service to Britwell from Windsor via Slough and Salt Hill, deviating from the main route at Farnham Road, 'The George'. (Ron Wellings)

Ex-RT1403 looks splendid with a fresh coat of paint following its transfer between members of the Ayrshire Bus Owners' consortium. It had been operated by member J.Murray since September 1956 and is now seen on 1st July of the year under review in Kilmarnock under the wing of Hill and Patterson. Withdrawn from service in March 1966 it was then cannibalized thus ending a career which extended from December 1948 when it first entered service with London Transport from Watford High Street garage. (A.J.Douglas)

RT4475, with a Saunders built body in place of its original Park Royal example, stands in the Minories Bus and Coach Station, Aldgate in brilliant summer sunshine. A fairly interesting career befell this bus during its period with London Transport. It had first entered service in March 1954 in Country Area livery with the body once carried by SRT123 but it spent its first few months operating from Central Area Twickenham garage. Moving on to Addlestone garage to commence its rightful sphere of operations in June 1954 it was to move to Crawley within the month. Upon its first overhaul in March 1958 it was outshopped in Central red bus livery and thereafter remained permanently in the Central Area although here it is ready for a trip to one of the more rural parts of that empire. (Ron Wellings)

Superb looking ex-RTL24 is running along South Beach, Ardrossan to its terminus at Clyde Terrace on 1st July. It had been acquired in August 1958 by the Ayrshire Bus Owners (A1) Service, owning member T.Hunter of Kilmarnock, via Bird's the Stratford-upon-Avon dealer. It carries body 4415 originally mounted on the chassis of RTL27. (A.J.Douglas)

Seen at the Lower Edmonton Station terminus of Route 128, Enfield's RT4075 with Weymann body waits to depart for Chase Farm Hospital. In 1969 of course this route was renumbered W8 and received the dreaded single deck MBS treatment. Behind the bus can be seen the old level crossing gates for the Edmonton Low Level line which was the original 1849 branch of the Northern & Eastern Railway between Shoreditch and Enfield Town via Angel Road, then called Water Lane. The final freight trains ran over this crossing in December 1964 and in the following year the track was lifted. (Ron Wellings)

Green Line liveried RT4494, in use on service 723B, exits Commercial Road at Aldgate East near the end of its journey followed by Camberwell's RTL1365 on its way to London Bridge on a short working of Route 40. The date is 1st September which was a Saturday, probably accounting for the peaceful nature of the scene. (Photofives)

The registration number JXC20 will always be remembered as that carried by the prototype RTL501, the Leyland equivalent of the RT. It was intended that the RTLs would be numbered following on from the five hundred eight feet wide Leylands, which accounts for the earliest delivered Leyland vehicle being given this fleet number. In the event however the wide vehicles were given a class designation (RTW) of their own. The Leyland chassis number 472471 was slotted into the Park Royal body building programme to materialise with the roof box body number 1936 and registration originally intended for RT657. Entering service in June 1948 it operated from Turnham Green garage and after two overhauls and use at three different garages it was delicensed in April 1958 still bearing its original body. Disposal to Bird's was in July 1958 when it was immediately acquired by A1 Service of Ardrossan. It is seen here at Saltcoats having had its roof box removed. (J.C.Walker)

Grays garage yard sometime during July reveals a line up of identical looking RTs. RT4037 showing details for Route 323B is nearest the camera; alongside RT1083 shows route number 368 one of the Bata Factory services; next in line RT3440 displays Route 374 details and furthest away is a Green Line liveried example, RT4492, with blinds set for Route 723A. Interestingly all the vehicles carry the original colour they had entered service with and are true Country Area stock. (Ron Wellings)

With the familiar Uxbridge branch of F.W.Woolworth & Co.Ltd. in the background, Weymann bodied RT291 shows the new order of double deck working on Route 224A. This became possible after 9th May with the lowering of the road under the railway bridge at High Road, Yiewsley. The bus returned to service from overhaul in September and the front advertisements herald the approach of Christmas. (Ron Wellings)

RT4303 with a via blind which still bears the scars of Route 64's cut back from Wimbledon Stadium in May of the previous year rests at the Tooting, Longmead Road stand. Note the advertisements carried on the front of the bus for the James Bond thriller, Dr.No, a film which some thirty plus years later is still dug out by the television programme planners on a fairly regular basis. (Ron Wellings)

RM368 is seen in Butterwick, Hammersmith in service to Tooting Station, Southern Region on Route 220. This route number had been reintroduced to the streets of London with the seventh stage of the trolleybus conversion programme on 20th July 1960 with Routemasters from Shepherds Bush garage. One of the initial batch to enter service at the time, the bus prepares to make the awkward filter manoeuvre into the traffic on its nearside at the end of the bus stop bays. (Alan Mortimer)

RTL1582 re-entered service at Shepherds Bush garage from its January overhaul and is seen here only a few days later substituting for an RM on the southern section of Route 220 at West Croydon. Delivered to the Executive in September 1954 it was not until March 1958 that it began to earn its keep, initially at Chelverton Road garage. (Ron Wellings)

This railway bridge at Mill Hill station clearly shows the necessity for the use of single deck vehicles on Route 240A. The construction of the southern extension of the M1 and the gloomy new bus station under the motorway enabled this crumbling brick arch to be replaced and for the first time double deckers could run through but this was still four years away. 1962 was the last year of passenger use for the TD class of vehicle and TD101 shows signs of neglect to its roof paintwork. Further use was found for this Leyland PS1 chassis fitted with Mann Egerton bodywork after disposal by London Transport and in April 1965 the 54th West Ham Scout Troop are recorded as its last owner. (F.W.Ivey)

RT3903 nears Morden Station at the end of the route while in use as CN5 on the 154 service. This reincarnation of the route number had appeared on 4th March 1959 with the first stage of the trolleybus replacement programme. Route 654 which had used trolleybuses with special braking systems to avoid run backs on Anerley Hill had the advantage of a very similar route number being available at the time of conversion. The trolleybuses of course had terminated at Sutton Green rather than Morden. The slip board on the front bulkhead points out that the bus passes near Crystal Palace Football Ground, not exactly a high flying club in 1962.
(Alan Mortimer)

At the southern tip of Hampstead Heath on 30th May all Leyland RTW16, fitted with the body first carried by RTW497, which it had received on its last overhaul in March of the year under review, now works out of Chalk Farm garage for the second time, having been a resident earlier for two years. Chalk Farm provided a small allocation to Route 45 but the lion's share came from Walworth. (John Gascoine)

During January RF543 was returned to Country Area service at Hemel Hempstead after a fifteen month extended loan to the Central Area where it worked from Kingston. Interestingly a two person crew are in use on a route which had been converted to OMO in June 1959. Whether this was due to a surfeit of conductors or the bus, which was supposedly converted for this type of operation in February 1959, not being properly fitted is uncertain. The brackets for the 'pay as you enter' board normally carried beneath the front nearside window have either been removed or maybe doubt remains as to when it was actually converted. An advertisement gained at Kingston has been removed from roof level. Later in this volume a further picture depicts the bus after it had been returned to service from its February overhaul. (Alan Mortimer)

Ex-RTL16 was used in passenger service by Stephenson's Motor Services of Bishop Auckland after acquisition in August 1958 from Bird's Commercial Motors, the dealer who initially purchased the vehicle from London Transport. Eventually in December 1966 it was withdrawn and cannibalised to provide spares but just now it is seen in smart external paint condition as it passes through Bishop Auckland with a reasonable passenger load on its journey to nearby Evenwood and West Auckland. Its existence was spread evenly, give or take a month or so, between its days operating within the capital and in the county of Durham, having first entered service in December 1948. (Alan Mortimer)

Seen passing through Kingston, RT564 carries the body first mounted on the chassis of RT490 and numbered 1739. The bus is working the full route through to Leatherhead on the hour and thirty five minute journey from Argyle Road at Ealing. In 1964 this bus would journey much further as deck cargo aboard ship to the island of Ceylon, now called Sri Lanka. (Alan Mortimer)

En-route for South Harrow station, RT2418 operates from Alperton garage and is seen passing down Acton Lane at Harlesden on 23rd April. It currently carries an RT8 body built by Weymann numbered 5223 which was first mounted on RT2344. This dismal background is typical of the immediate industrial area bounded by the railway between Willesden Junction and Stonebridge Park with the Grand Union Canal to the south and which once included the Park Royal Coachworks factory. (Roger Partridge)

Route 34B, which was a Monday to Friday rush hour only operation and worked at its fullest extent between Brimsdown Power Station and the Crooked Billet at Walthamstow, originated in March 1918 when journeys on Route 76 were extended down Angel Road to the Cartridge Factory. Two months later they went further along to Aerator's Works. In 1924 these journeys were numbered 167 and in October 1934 they became 34B. The buses worked off the 76 route and it was rare for a Tottenham conductor to re-set the blinds correctly. Here RTW147 in Green Street still wears its 76 dress apart from the front route number blind and the destination which relate to its 34B activity. Looking in good shape this bus can be seen being delivered to Tottenham from Aldenham in the 1961 book of this series. (Alan Mortimer)

RT3001 is seen operating the circular route 173 with Peckham Rye Common in the background as it turns into the road of the same name at the 'King's Arms' public house. Only Nunhead Lane is shown on the via points blind, the simplicity intended to make it clear which way round the bus was working on the outward leg of its journey from Peckham garage. Rostered duty PM1 is carried by this Park Royal bodied vehicle which in October 1964 was withdrawn from service to be exported to Cape Town before the year came to a close. (Roger Partridge)

RML892 was photographed at North Finchley on 28th August with several month's passenger use now completed on Route 104. It is seen travelling from Barnet to the City terminus at Finsbury Square, Moorgate on what appears to be a very warm day. This particular bus can now be found in the Cowie South London fleet working from Brixton garage. (Tom Smith)

Just a reminder of better times with RTL696 passing through the main gates of Aldenham Overhaul Works with its stylish brick built pillar and totem on 5th June. Leaving the works after its third overhaul and now carrying Metro-Cammell body number 4078, it would re-enter service from Clapton garage. In June 1966 it was delicensed and transferred to Loughton, moving on to Poplar in January 1967 with a further move to Hornchurch in February 1967 still delicensed where it stayed until disposed of in September. (John Gascoine)

RT1327 leaves Aldenham Works on 5th March bound for further service at Upton Park having just been overhauled. It now carries Saunders built body number 2648 of the same batch, numbered 2431 to 2680, with which it had first entered service in March 1950 at Croydon garage. In the background Chalk Farm staff bus RTL367 journeys along the roadway to the works. (John Gascoine)

London Transport maintained a tenuous link with West Wycombe by means of Route 455A. Technically it ran from Wooburn Common via Holtspur and High Wycombe but operated in two unconnected sections split at the latter place apart from an odd journey through to Beaconsfield. Even then there were at most three journeys a day on either section and no Sunday service. Here roof box RT648 carrying the body once mounted on the chassis of RT996 nears the end of its 13 minute journey from West Wycombe and a driver sees the chance of a lift into the garage. This bus was delicensed for the last time in November 1963 and eventually joined the ever expanding fleet of ex-London Transport vehicles operating in Ceylon. (Ron Wellings)

Standing opposite Leatherhead garage RT4767 awaits a new crew before finishing the last leg of its journey from Kingston to Bookham Station via Preston Cross. Only having re-entered service a few days earlier from its June overhaul it now carries body number 9008 from sister RT4766. (Ron Wellings)

RT1596 journeys through Catford on its way to Waterloo complete with a Guinness advertisement which requires a second glance to fully appreciate. A slipboard announcing 'To & From Farnborough Hospital' is carried for this weekday service, visitors on Sunday needing to use the extended 47 or 51 routes. In its original condition with a Park Royal body this bus had the distinction of being the lowest numbered RT to be delivered new lacking the upper deck cream relief around the windows. Morphy Richards, the electrical appliance manufacturer, were to become the new owners when the bus was disposed of in May 1963. (Alan Mortimer)

This is Eden Street, Kingston immediately following the last stage of the trolleybus to diesel bus conversion programme. Trolleybus wiring now hangs unwanted and unused awaiting the contractors to move in and dismantle the last vestige of a system which once operated over 256 miles of the capital's roads. RM1200 was one of the initial batch to be allocated to Norbiton garage for its involvement in the conversion. 283 was the weekday replacement route for 603 working in from Tolworth to traverse the Kingston loop clockwise which is carefully described on the via point blind while the destination is an end to end display. The anti-clockwise loop was worked by the 282 from the Dittons which also covered both directions on a Sunday. (Dave Berwick)

Reigate garage's RF614 lays over on Route 440A with a few passengers having been allowed to board. First entering service in July 1953 from Dorking garage it was transferred to Hertford some four years later and arrived at Reigate following overhaul in April of the year under review. (Alan Mortimer)

Heading south from Potters Bar on Barnet Road, Stevenage garaged RF161 has
the greater part of its journey on Route 716A to accomplish before arrival at its
destination of Woking. But for the modern lampposts that have been erected and
the parked cars the background scene seems to be caught in a time warp.
(Alan Mortimer)

The 98A route, originally introduced in 1952 on weekdays between Hounslow garage and Pinner, had gone through
many changes in the intervening ten years. By 1962 it was running on Monday-Friday from Hounslow to
Hillingdon Station extended to Ruislip in the rush hours and on Sunday from Hounslow to North Harrow Station.
Here RT4158 rests on a wet Sunday at North Harrow before journeying to Hounslow as UX3. An earlier roof box
Park Royal body now replaces the original Weymann non-roof box version. (Alan Mortimer)

RT4392 operating from Merton garage passes West Croydon Station on Route 157 as it journeys to Crystal Palace on 14th April. Croydon is constantly changing but this corner of Station Road survives although opposite is the site of the present West Croydon bus station. (Roger Partridge)

RLH52 was originally delivered in green livery and entered service from Guildford garage in November 1953. Repainted into Central Area colours together with RLH7, 29 and 49 in April 1959 they were subsequently housed at Dalston for use on Route 178. Harrow Weald then operated this RLH before it moved back into the Country Area in May 1962 to cover while other green members of the class went through their third overhaul cycle. Seen here in Redhill still in red it is in use on the weekday short workings of Route 447 which ran to South Merstham, Manor Road rather than the further destination of Delabole Road. (Alan Mortimer)

Not officially but very frequently RLH's worked the new route 230A from Harrow Weald garage. Seen in Kenton Lane, RLH62 carries the remarkably informative proper blind which was odd since by this time a 'lazy' end to end blind had been introduced for the longer 230 route. First entering service in December 1952 this RLH managed sixteen plus years serving Londoners before being delicensed in June 1969 to be sold in December for a new life in the U.S.A. (Ron Wellings)

Standing within Sevenoaks Bus Station Dunton Green garaged RT3149 displays a destination blind for Chipstead, the northern terminus of Route 454. The southern point reached was Tonbridge although it appears that this journey on duty DG2 is a short working from Sevenoaks. The bus stand number 4 lists routes 413, 413A and 454 in the Chipstead direction and intending passengers are provided with a flimsy metal queue barrier. An RF of the original private hire type stands at right angles in a farther corner of the bus station. (Kevin Lane)

RTL474 is seen in alien territory while in use on the special service operating between Southfields Station and Wimbledon tennis grounds some distance from its usual haunts, being a Willesden garaged vehicle. There appears to be a total lack of tennis fans and traffic and the policeman on point duty looks as though he is wondering where they have all got to. (Alan Mortimer)

This fine example of a small normal control bus was photographed on 27th April, some twenty seven years after first entering service with the LPTB as their fleet number C54b. General deterioration is much in evidence but it is after all some seventeen years since initial disposal to the Belgian Economic Mission as one of a batch of thirty to make the short sea crossing to the continent. At sometime in its exile it has been given a public service registration number, the letter P indicating this within its newer identification 8821P. Now owned by Paul Pironet of Pepinster, near Verviers, it is seen parked on land which purports to be the owner's garage at Pepinster and is carrying route information relevant to it being on hire to Belgium Railways and used in service on a route operating between Pepinster and Trooz. (D.A.Jones)

Travelling south through Harpenden RF184, garaged at Luton, would appear that it still has to pick up its passengers for a visit to the circus now performing at Olympia. In the background a Vauxhall Velox is parked in front of two well known high street stores, Boots and Sainsburys. This would have been one of those old fashioned Sainsbury stores where you queued to be served at each individual counter and in 1962 the supermarket with its checkouts was only beginning to proliferate. (Alan Mortimer)

Route 270 was introduced as a 'suburbanised' section of Route 27 from Kensington to Teddington Station in May 1956 and lasted as such until February 1963. On 14th April Hammersmith garaged RTL448 traverses Chiswick High Road. The Depot Dining Rooms adjacent to the Chiswick Works entrance obviously sought to offer an alternative menu to the famous Chiswick canteen. This bus was one of a number which paid a visit to the Aldenham Works in February 1965 for the express purpose of having its Weymann body, 8677, removed and replaced by an older example, 5328, before its disposal to the Ceylon Transport Board in September of the same year. (Roger Partridge)

The background with the 1950s architecture of Peckham garage is now but a memory with the demolition and clearing of the site during the early months of 1997. In times when the building's permanence seemed unquestionable RT1173 of nearby Rye Lane garage waits to take up duties on Route 37 to Hounslow garage. Sadly the RT had an even shorter period in the ownership of London Transport than the garage being disposed of in April 1963 to Arlington Motors, bus and coach dealers of Ponders End. However you view the situation nowadays this RT lives on having been renumbered RT190 and re-registered HLX177 some years after it had moved into the preservation movement. The body carried in this picture and at the time of withdrawal is actually that originally mounted on RT190. (Alan Mortimer)

Weekday Route 230A was introduced on 10th October providing a service to College Avenue and College Hill Road at Harrow Weald and was allocated two RTs although more often than not it made use of RLH buses from Route 230. Here however an immaculate RT1954, Harrow Weald's latest acquisition after overhaul at Aldenham in August works the route with the first autumn leaves beginning to fall. In August the following year the route was reduced to peak hours only and in January 1966 it was withdrawn in favour of a peak hour extension of 209 to cover. (Ron Wellings)

RT3036 had been demoted to learner duties in November 1961 and here on 17th June it is seen still in use in this temporary role while taking a rest inside Shepherds Bush garage. It returned to passenger use at Abbey Wood garage in February 1963. In the background and enhanced with the same Black & White whisky advertisement, RTL371, in use as a staff bus since October 1959, stands ready for its next outing. The unmistakable rear of the newest type to join the London Transport bus fleet in the shape of an RM stands on the extreme left of the picture. (John Gascoine)

New route 380 had been introduced in 1961 to replace the section of Route 388 between Hertford and Sawbridgeworth. At Hertford bus station, with the familiar cafe in the background, GS5 departs for the extremity of the route which had seven return journeys on weekdays and four on Sundays. In October the bus was delicensed and stored at Grays garage, being sold the following September to Hipperson's Supplies Ltd. a contractor of Dagenham being the only example to be owned. Sadly it was scrapped in 1975 after having passed through the hands of a small number of owners. (Alan Mortimer)

When photographed on 26th April RM838 was just nine months into its long life and at the time this book was being prepared the bus was in service with Reading Mainline hiding under the re-registered number XYJ440. It is seen in Egerton Road at one end of which stands Stamford Hill garage from where it first operated in July 1961 with the ninth stage of the trolleybus conversion programme. Upper case lettering was still in use for via point blinds when the Stamford Hill routes were converted but they were lovingly cared for and remained in use here for many years after less careful garages had received lower case replacements. (John Gascoine)

Seen emerging from the Butterwick bus station at Hammersmith, Stevenage based RF163 rejoins the main stream of traffic as it continues its journey to Woking on Green Line Route 716A. The date is 14th April and the well loaded coach on this sunny day probably gives relief from lower temperatures judging by the well wrapped up cyclist who eyes the photographer while signalling his intentions to the traffic behind. (Roger Partridge)

After only a bare six months of operation the Saturday service of Route 292 was withdrawn and replaced by new Route 292A. Operating the same roads as the 292 from Borehamwood to Burnt Oak it then turned north instead of south and went to Edgware Station no longer serving Colindale. At its home garage bus station RT2869 working duty EW2 waits departure for Borehamwood, Rossington Avenue. (Ron Wellings)

Twickenham's RT188, now fitted with a Weymann body, had originally entered service in October 1947 with a Park Royal built example of similar appearance. Now nearing the end of its operational life with London Transport it is seen on Route 71 which had been introduced in January 1950 as a service to connect Richmond and Kingston with the Ham Estate roads. By 1962 East Acton had become the northern terminus and on a Saturday the route had been extended beyond Kingston to Sunbury Station. (Alan Mortimer)

One month into its ownership with the Hamsters Mobile Theatre Group of London, E6, ex-RT89, still in LT red, travels at speed through the countryside on the South Mimms by-pass now part of the M25. Although always a target for vandals, as was the STD bus it replaced, it accomplished several year's service in its new role before being withdrawn early in 1967. The Group's latest production 'Conversations in a Wood' is carried neatly in the front via box aperture while close examination of the original print reveals the company's name in the destination box. (John Gascoine)

This version of Route 60 came into being in October 1961 when Route 260 was renumbered and was to last only until September 1968. Initially it worked between Cricklewood Garage and Waterloo on Mondays to Fridays with a peak hour extension to Surrey Docks. RT1743, showing a loss of paint at roof level, waits at the Waterloo bus stand. This vehicle was taken out of service the following year, eventually giving a further two year's service to B.Davenport of Netherton before being scrapped in 1965. (Kevin Lane)

Although in green livery RT2252 spent its first two months of passenger use in the Central Area from February 1949 operating from Mortlake garage. It was eventually transferred to its rightful area of operation to be garaged at Northfleet. Upon its return to service after its August 1960 overhaul one could be forgiven for thinking it was a new delivery with unblemished bodywork free from advertising material and now carrying Green Line fleetname and motif. Allocated to Swanley Junction it is seen at Eccleston Bridge in October performing its proper duties. (Tony R.Packer)

Service vehicle 400W was disposed of to W.North of Leeds in April 1960 and languished in their scrapping fields for some considerable time. On 20th January of the year under review, somewhat distorted and in company with a variety of other vehicles, it awaits its final fate, although even here it still proves useful to hold some engine units. The chassis used for this 6½ ton towing lorry had originally been mounted with a Weymann coach body with seating for 30 and was used on Green Line work when it first entered service in January 1931 as T246. With the delivery of new coaches later in the decade the batch T207 through to T306 were withdrawn from this type of work and some, including this chassis, were converted for service vehicle use. (John Gascoine)

Seen traversing the countryside near Ludlow on 27th July, ex-GS49 now belongs to the Corvedale Motor Co.Ltd. as their fleet number 8. Previously it had spent its entire LT passenger operating service from November 1953 to November 1958 at Northfleet garage. (A.J.Douglas)

In Green Line colour scheme RT3228 carries no advertising to mar its appearance, which was the normal practice for this elite branch of London Transport. This was to change the following year when for the first time advertising appeared on the lower deck rear end panels of the double deck coach fleet. Alongside Poplar garaged RM98 in use on Route 23 lays over before returning to Becontree Heath. (Tom Smith)

On 15th April 'Diddler' trolleybus number 1 stands next to RM50, which was at the time acting as a trainer garaged at West Ham. The unmistakable spacious yard at Fulwell, still with the tramway track of 1902 in place, is the setting for this specially posed view. Nearly thirty years in the development of road passenger transport is represented here with the trolleybus having first entered service with London United Tramways in February 1931. The bus was delivered in September 1959 to commence its career with a chequered start either as a learner, unlicensed in store or in short spells of passenger use until it eventually settled down to a normal existence three years later garaged at Stonebridge. Its life was cut short in 1973 in a garage fire at Walworth. (Ron Wellings)

On Saturday 30th June RTL22 travels east along an almost deserted Old Street on its journey to Leyton Green on Route 170. Clapton garage housed this bus, the second lowest numbered RTL left in London passenger service in 1962. For a few months in 1967 it had the honour of being the lowest number after the sale of RTL19. (John Gascoine)

A watery scene at Edgware Station features RT2926, a Cricklewood garaged bus, in use on Route 266 substituting for an RM. Also seen is RM512 working Route 18, while behind the haphazardly placed Route 18 dolly stop RM866 appears to be the next bus to depart. The RT and RM blinds for Route 266 make an interesting comparison with four extra pieces of information included on the RT. (Ron Wellings)

RT4563 stands at the Uxbridge terminus of Route 321 with destination blind set for St.Albans LT garage as at that period no journeys on the route from Uxbridge worked right through to Luton, such workings starting at Maple Cross. First entering service from North Street, Romford garage it was returned to service following its first overhaul in May 1957 wearing Country Area colours and allocated to St.Albans garage. Having passed around a number of Country Area garages it eventually reached Garston after its January 1962 overhaul. (Ron Wellings)

As well as new Routemasters, Stonebridge garage received several early RMs which had previously been used as trainers when they converted from trolleybuses on 3rd January. RM48 was one such example although it returned to training duties at West Ham before the month was out. Nevertheless an SE garage code has been painted on the bodywork and here it heads north at Craven Park on new Route 266. Three members of staff congregate at one of the doorways to the London Transport establishment which provided refreshment and comfort facilities for staff changing duties from SE and it also displayed a clock which presumably showed official LT time. (Alan Mortimer)

Route 76 was served by the RTW class for many years and RTW228 lays over at the short working Stoke Newington terminus before returning to Victoria. Upton Park, Putney Bridge, Dalston and lastly Tottenham were the only garages to which this bus was allocated. In November 1965 it was delicensed and put into store at Walthamstow and then moved to Poplar before being despatched to Ceylon in January 1966. The latest Plaza Cinema showing is the film 'A Girl Named Tamiko' which starred among others Laurence Harvey, France Nuyen and Martha Hyer. (John Gascoine)

In 1962 RTs still maintained the Green Line services in East London and on 21st April RT3251 waits in the Minories Bus and Coach Station at Aldgate before its return journey to Corbets Tey at Upminster on the 722 route. Certain journeys on this route operated to Hornchurch Station but these were to disappear in July. (Roger Partridge)

In three years time RTW128 would be disposed of in the first mass sales of the class. It was to be exported to Canada to begin a fulfilling second life on the far side of the Atlantic. Here in 1962 however it is seen pulling into the Butterwick bus stands at Hammersmith as it journeys to Mortlake garage on Route 9, being one of the fourteen which Dalston provided for the service on a Saturday. (Alan Mortimer)

On 14th April Holloway garaged RT1262 with a Park Royal built body in place of its original Saunders example journeys along Chiswick High Road approaching the London Transport works. Trolleybus wiring for Routes 657 and 667 is strung across the road but withdrawal of these two services is now only just over a month away after which time new bus route 267 and extensions to established routes 81B, 116 and 117 will join the 27 in running past this motley array of shops. (Roger Partridge)

Sidcup garaged RT2428 is showing a via point blind for the full Monday to Friday working on Route 228 from Surrey Docks. However the bus is turning into the approach road to the Well Hall Station terminus at Eltham with blind already set for its return to the Gordon Arms at Chislehurst. An RT can be seen following the 228 into the terminus from Well Hall Road on Route 195, a route we have found to be strangely camera shy. (Ron Wellings)

Having just passed under the railway bridge with East Dulwich station out of view to the left and Dog Kennel Hill rising in the background, RTL664 journeys to Greenwich on the horseshoe shaped route 185. The wide expanse of the four tram tracks have disappeared long ago and mature shrubs now mark the dual carriageway of the notorious incline which the bus has just descended. The date is 13th April and this Walworth garaged bus has just re-entered service after its overhaul of the same month. The Southern Electric notice above the bridge names a selection of destinations ending with the rather vague statement 'and other Surrey Hills stations'. (Roger Partridge)

RTL1631 was the highest numbered of the class being delivered to the Executive in November 1954 although it did not enter passenger service until December 1958. Dalston garage had the honour to provide a home for the Weymann bodied bus until its initial visit to Aldenham for overhaul in March 1962. It re-entered service operating from Clapton garage and on 30th June stands crewless in Dove Road, the stand for journeys terminating at Mildmay Park. There are no exterior blemishes visible on the well maintained 1950 built Park Royal body, 3498, which was first carried by RTL463. (John Gascoine)

Nearing its sad end is ex-RTL37 which had suffered fire damage while in the ownership of J.Laurie, trading as Chieftain and it is now dumped at Bird's Commercial Motors' premises at Stratford-upon-Avon. It gradually deteriorated over the years and with exterior panelling removed provides an insight into some of the construction methods used by Park Royal in the building of this body, numbered 2234, which had initially graced the chassis of RTL13. One of the remains of the other buses is definitely ex-Birmingham and the sports car in the foreground was presumably someone's prized possession once upon a time. (Alan Mortimer)

With the canopy of West Croydon station just protruding into the picture, RT4521 stands on the opposite side of Station Road as it departs for Horsham via Crawley as specified on the destination blind which doesn't trust the passenger to read the via point blind above. Having received an overhaul in August of the year under review, the bus now carries body number 6048 which had been initially fitted to RT3167. (Ron Wellings)

'Q1035', or 1035CD as it was properly known, is seen on 28th January, inside Tottenham garage which was its normal place of residence. This vehicle was unique among the service vehicle fleet being the only conversion carried out on a Q class bus and was to an 8 seat mobile gas unit used as a support vehicle for the London Transport Civil Defence Corps. Originally Q75, first entering service in October 1935, it was withdrawn from normal passenger work in August 1952 for its transformation although it retained its Country Area green livery. It also kept its original fleet number until the rather incorrect service vehicle number was substituted in May 1954. The bus survived in this mode until July 1964 when it was disposed of to Lammas Motors of London SW17. (John Gascoine)

RM767 was allocated to Edmonton from April 1961 through to its first visit to Aldenham for overhaul in November 1965. Monday to Friday route 279A operated between Flamstead End and Tottenham Hale or Tottenham Garage in the evenings and came into being with stage 10 of the trolleybus conversion programme on 26th April 1961. It provided a service down to the factory area at the Hale and also a north-south through service at Waltham Cross which was beyond the capabilities of the trolleybuses. Here the bus pulls away from the stop at Tramway Avenue heading south. (Alan Mortimer)

Although RM production had only reached RM1282 the first of the order for sixty eight Green Line coach variants, RMC1453, was delivered from Park Royal on 28th June three weeks ahead of the first batch. As seen in this picture the coaches had double headlamps on each side of the radiator grille and a revised layout of blind apertures with no provision for a separate route number blind. RMC1461 is seen at Park Royal works with presumably an odd blind inserted to check the dimensions and working mechanism.

On 12th August RTW355 is seen traversing Regent Street as it journeys to the Aldwych by way of Route 6. Now the regular terminus of the route, in 1962 this was only the halfway point. Last overhauled in June 1961 the bus now carries the body originally mounted on the chassis of RTW283. The class of five hundred buses conveniently given body numbers 2901 through to 3400 were built by Leyland and the entire complement were known as 6RT6. Interestingly they were originally to be coded 1/4RT1/4 after a delivery of eight feet wide RT class vehicles with the classification 4RT4 which in the event never materialised. (Ron Wellings)

On 15th September RTL22 stands alongside the tram tracks last used in 1939 in the forecourt of Clapton garage paying scant heed to the prohibition on the dolly stop. It is blinded for the Clapton Greyhound Special between Clapton Pond and Clapton Stadium, a distance of just over half a mile. Hardly worth waiting for the bus one would think but perhaps this was a 6d luxury you might afford if you had enjoyed a good evening at the dogs. (John Gascoine)

Edgware garage's only incursion into the central London scene was its Sunday allocation on Route 52, on which day a through service was operated from Rossington Avenue at Borehamwood to Victoria. Their RT1247 heads a line of buses in the 52 bay at Victoria Station on a wet and deserted Sunday. The driver's failure to move his bus up has caused the access to the adjacent 25 bay to become blocked, doubtless to the annoyance of that route's drivers. (Ron Wellings)

Attempts are obviously being made to smarten up the exterior of ex-RT1436 now rust-ridden after seven years service with London Transport and six with the Ayrshire Bus Owners (A1) Service. Kerr & Linney, the owning members, have only altered the bus to a minimal degree having merely repanelled the offside route number plate holder and removed the running duty plate bracketing. Seen at Dreghorn, which is located just south east of Irvine, on 2nd July while on service to Ardrossan via Dalry Road and Beggs Terrace the bus is now just thirteen months away from being withdrawn as fleet number 12A in August 1963. (A.J.Douglas)

Entering Barking garage from Longbridge Road, RT545 is now in its last year of public service with the Executive, being withdrawn from service in January 1963 although not disposed of until the following January. Route 23 worked at its fullest extent between Marylebone Station and Becontree Heath but for this tired old lady the garage is more inviting than the Heath on this BK3 duty. (Alan Mortimer)

RTL1357 on Route 2 from Cricklewood garage negotiates Hyde Park Corner with the long term road alterations still in progress. A typical London taxi of the period follows closely behind while a Vauxhall saloon of the Cresta and Velox style completes the trio making headway past the construction debris. Having first entered service in December 1952, Cricklewood was to be the last home for this bus prior to its disposal. (Alan Mortimer)

RTL487 has just entered Eversholt Street from the junction with Euston Road on 23rd December heading for Chalk Farm on Route 68 with no Euston bus station to deflect its progress. The bus is fitted with Park Royal body number 9105 which would later be removed and exchanged for an earlier example, number 3442, before disposal in September 1965. A 'To and From The Old Vic' slipboard is carried beneath the canopy while another famous landmark looms behind in the shape of St.Pancras parish church. (John Gascoine)

Former B7 was disposed of by London Transport still fitted with its Park Royal body in January 1953 having initially entered service in June 1942 on route 97 garaged at Hanwell (HW). It was acquired by Crosville Motor Services of Chester to enter service in March 1953 with fleet number MB166. In November 1954 it was rebodied with a 1948 built ECW lowbridge body which it still carries in this picture taken during the early summer of the year now under review. The fleet number, DKA166, was applied in May 1958. Further use was made of the vehicle by the Atomic Power Construction (Trawsfynydd) Ltd. when disposed of by Crosville later in the year under review and it was scrapped in November 1964 after completing nearly twelve years service with three operators. A nice Bedford OB coach, registered JC9712, operating for White Way is parked further along the road. (Ron Wellings)

At Stratford Broadway the significant 'A' on this RM's route number blind is far from clear. This Saturday only 238A route was introduced on 14th October 1961 while RM16 found itself once again operating from West Ham in April of the year under review having spent some months of unlicensed activity at various north London garages after a first period at the garage near the Greengate. The Monday to Friday 238 from Little Heath went to Canning Town and North Woolwich rather than Stratford while the Sunday service from Stratford to Little Heath was provided by 162A which went a different way at Upton Park. Confused ? - I'll bet the residents of Little Heath were! (Ron Wellings)

Ex-GS32 dates from November 1953 when it first entered service with London Transport from Dunton Green garage on the 471, their only route which utilised this 26 seat OMO type of vehicle. After its one and only overhaul in January 1957 it re-entered service from Epping, moving on to Guildford, Amersham, East Grinstead, Dorking and finally Swanley Junction before being delicensed and stored. Its last few months were spent gathering dust at Romford, London Road garage before eventual sale to Bird's of Stratford-upon-Avon in June 1961 and then to R.B.Talbott who traded as Barry's Coaches at Moreton-in-Marsh. Nowadays the bus is owned by John Clarke who has brought it back to full LT condition, a major task when one considers that its use before moving into the preservation sphere was as a farm shed. (Alan Mortimer)

Horsham station buildings provide the background to RT2517 resting between duties on the lengthy route 414, the northern terminus of which was at West Croydon. Horsham was the most southerly point reached by London Transport bus operations in 1962 and the Southdown Leyland bus speeding into the picture on the left illustrates the other major operator who served the area. Upon its next visit to Aldenham the RT, as well as receiving an overhaul, would be outshopped in Central Area livery thus bringing to an end a long association with Reigate garage where it would complete eight years of passenger service. (Roy Marshall)

RT2496 was eventually to be exported to France in May 1968 after an active career from initial entry into service in January 1950 at Forest Gate garage. It was to be used at New Cross, Cricklewood and Harrow Weald garages and receive two overhauls before its sale in September 1962. Aspec Travel Ltd., dealers of Ilford, immediately acquired the bus and it entered service with Super Coaches of Upminster before the end of the month. Seen on 20th October at Hornchurch in a revised livery but still with LT advertising, it operates on Route 8 between there and County Park Estate. This was one of a small number of independent routes working in this area at the time. The bus later passed to the Executors of S.Ledgard, Armley until they were acquired by the West Yorkshire Road Car Co.Ltd. who did not operate any of Ledgard's ex-London vehicles.

This interesting scene taken inside Gillingham Street, Victoria garage on 17th June depicts normal residents with intruders from the Standerwick, Blackpool fleet enjoying a wash and brush up before returning up north. RTL1132 showing damage to both front wheel arches together with a typical front nearside roof dent appears ready for service when called upon. RF22 is the emergency replacement coach for any Green Line vehicle which finds itself in difficulties in the Central London area and shows the one line route blind fitted which covered all coach services. At the moment it can't decide if 717 (London, Victoria) or 718 (Windsor) is what is needed beneath its Green Line motif. (John Gascoine)

The 225 between Eastcote Lane and Northwood was one of the more obscure routes in the Central Area. Starting with one man operated Cubs in January 1944 it graduated to Ts four months later and was double decked in 1946 when it ventured north of the original terminus at Northwood Hills to Northwood. The only other change came in 1957 when a Sunday afternoon extension to Mount Vernon Hospital was introduced. Finally in 1963 it was absorbed into Route 232. Two of the buses on the route were photographed on a day in Autumn 1962 and serve to show the gradual infiltration of lower case lettering on via point blinds. RT1598 above has a new display while RT814 below soldiers on with the style introduced in 1955. (Ron Wellings)

Rush hour only Route 248A operated between Upminster Station and Corbets Tey and was introduced in 1959 in recognition of an over zealous cut in facilities in 1958. Previously the 249 route had run between these points and was a favourite source of trivia as the shortest Central Area route although latterly it did gain an extension to Upminster Park Estate. An attempt to cover the withdrawal by an extension of 250 failed and 248A was the result. RLH59 as duty RD110 waits at Upminster Station for the expected rush of commuters in this summer scene. (Ron Wellings)

By now well established, Route 239 which operated between its City terminus of Moorgate seen here and Hampstead Heath was one of five new motor bus routes introduced on 1st February 1961 and operated by the old Holloway trolleybus depot called 'Highgate' garage for convenience. RM618 was one of the huge number of RMs which first entered service with the scheme and now on 28th August of the year under review is beginning to look a little mature. (Tom Smith)

RT1173 travels north on the approaches to Vauxhall Bridge on 29th September. This panoramic scene emphasises yet another road junction which is now completely changed with only the Vauxhall station buildings standing above the road intersection as a present day identifying feature. The RT was disposed of in April of the following year and is documented as having an identity problem after it had moved into the preservation movement in 1970, masquerading as another RT in later years. (Henry Heyworth)

Garston garage on 5th June provided the visitor with a fine assortment of vehicles including RT3650 and RT3425. Nearest the camera RT3650 is still dressed from its previous use on express route 803 which operated between Uxbridge and Welwyn Garden City at its fullest extent. Note the minimum fare of 9d board carried beneath the canopy. The further RT again shows Garston LT garage as its destination having worked in from Route 311, a Shenley to Leavesden operation. The roof box example departed for Ceylon in May 1964 while the scrapping fields of Wombwell in February 1977 was the last destination for the other bus. (John Gascoine)

Two RTs, 1314 on the left and 4234 on the right, stand at Edgware Station on Route 114 on 21st July. The bodies of both vehicles were originally products of the Saunders company on Anglesey but RT1314 now carries a Weymann body, number 1706. RT4234 carries an earlier Saunders body, number 2485, than that it had originally owned and which it had gained at overhaul in March. RT1314 was disposed of in February 1963 while June 1978 was the date RT4234 eventually left London to be scrapped at Wombwell. (John Gascoine)

Another example of the fairly rapid introduction of lower case lettered via point blinds is shown here by RT4093 which has just re-entered service from its September overhaul with an RT8 Weymann body number 6801. The scene is Tooting Broadway, the terminus point for several routes including the 80 group. Shepherds Bush garaged RM325 is merely passing through on its journey to West Croydon Station from Harlesden on Route 220. An interesting comparison of some of the shop facades and the total lack of any reminder of the trams or trolleybuses which once operated along this stretch of road can be observed by referring back to the upper picture on page 66 of the 1952 book of this series. (Ron Wellings)

On 7th April RT1035 waits as passengers board and alight beneath trolleybus wiring at the Red Lion, Tolworth before continuing on its journey to Tadworth via Merland Rise. The slipboard carried beneath the canopy giving detailed information relating to minimum fares is not quite distinguishable but the fares quoted are 6d and 8d, the lower of which equates to 2½p! This bus had originally entered service in Country Area green but in May 1965 along with a number of others during that year received red livery for transfer to the Central Area. (Alan B.Cross)

It is interesting to compare this picture of an RM on Route 256 at Finsbury Square, Moorgate with that on page 94 of the 1961 book of this series. The trolleybus wires have been removed and so too have the rather elegant Georgian residences behind the bus. Only gaping fireplaces remain here on 28th August and doubtless faceless office premises will soon fill in the gap. In this picture RM233 from Walthamstow is working the innovative route which served the Millfields Estate at Clapton and provided new links to the City from Blackhorse Road and Higham Hill. (Tom Smith)

During October Epping and Windsor became the second garages to receive an allocation of the new RMC type of coach and routes 718, 720 and 720A were converted. At Aldgate in December RMC1478 waits to depart for Bishops Stortford with the remains of a recent snowfall in evidence. This route had been reduced to an hourly frequency when the double deckers were introduced. RT4498 with blinds rewound for its return journey to Tilbury Ferry on service 723B stands behind. (Alan Mortimer)

RT1822 is seen in Willow Walk as it heads into West Green garage which can be seen on the left. The building, which dated from 1925, was closed on 3rd January and its involvement with Route 29A would be transferred to Palmers Green. This RT is on a very short loan to West Green prior to its transfer to Wood Green and judging by the atrocious road conditions the sight of refuge is welcomed by the driver. (A.B.Cross)

The Palace Theatre in Clarendon Road, Watford has just been passed by RF543 on its journey from the Junction to Hemel Hempstead, Highfield on Route 322. The route had been extended within the Highfield area on 17th January from the former terminus at Bathurst Road to Deimos Drive and ran further on peak hour journeys to the Rotax factory on Maylands Avenue. This Metro-Cammell bus first entered service in April 1953 from St.Albans garage. (Alan B.Cross)

RM203 entered passenger service in February 1960 at West Ham garage, being part of the large allocation required with stage six of the trolleybus conversion programme. It was to continue in residence at this garage until its first visit to Aldenham in January 1964 for overhaul and is seen at Stratford Broadway on the Sunday only Route 162A. This suffixed number had been introduced in the complicated October 1961 changes when the weekday service on 162 had been re-routed to Mayesbrook Park. (Ron Wellings)

RT2476 re-entered service at Bromley garage from its May overhaul and is seen in company with two other RTs including Sidcup's RT1397 awaiting departure time at Well Hall Station. Very long standing route 61 is still a common sight to this day operating over the section between Chislehurst and Bromley. The further RT is in use on the 51B route which only operated to Well Hall during Monday to Friday peak hours and in this form was withdrawn after the last day of June 1964. Cinema advertising is prominent and 'Call Me Bwana' and 'Who's Got the Action' are advertised - anyone remember them? (R.H.G.Simpson)

Looking undressed without its front bumper, GS35 is soon to depart on 1st April from the Onslow Street bus station at Guildford for a journey to Peaslake on Route 448. In 1962 the route was still operated jointly with the Tillingbourne Valley Services and this continued until the last involvement with the route by London Transport arrived on 11th August 1964 after which the route returned solely to its 1924 originator. From this date the type of vehicle did not change but the maroon livery of Tillingbourne reigned supreme. When in January 1968 GS35 was sold by London Transport it found a new use as a van complete with a rear roller door and was used by H.Lotery & Co.Ltd. a manufacturer in Newport, Monmouthshire. (W.R.Legg)

On a rare sunny day very early in the year Hounslow garage bus station finds RT812 together with RT2950 waiting for their next trips to Greenford and Bedfont. Since August 1959 Weymann built body number 1817 has been carried by RT812 leading to its sale in September 1964. The original chassis to carry this body, RT568, was not disposed of until 1978. An unusual though not unique use was afforded RT812 very soon after its sale when it appeared in the French made film 'Allez-France' re-registered 333-QP-75 and it was then used for advertising the production. (Ron Wellings)

The date is 23rd July and in Grays RT4749 is seen en-route for Uplands Estate on one of the cross town services. Initially delivered to the Executive in April 1954 entry of the bus into service was delayed until April 1958. After use at Amersham and Hertford an overhaul at Aldenham was carried out in December 1961. Re-entering service at Dunton Green a few days loan to Godstone followed before transfer to Grays garage in January of the year under review. The bus now faces a period working among the uninspiring scenery of this Thames side area. Typical of the period is the 1950s tubular steel bus shelter of which two can be seen - a far cry from the 'Adshel' variety now so common throughout the land. (Ron Wellings)

RM49 had seen sporadic use in passenger service since initial delivery in September 1959 with two months at Tottenham in service on routes 76 and 34B as its initiation to the rigours of what lay ahead. Further short periods in its intended role occurred in April 1960 with operation at Walthamstow in connection with the sixth stage of the trolleybus conversion programme and again at Stonebridge Park garage with the 13th stage which took place in January of the year under review. Since that brief foray in north-west London it has once again returned to learner and familiarisation duties and on 9th June is parked at West Ham garage awaiting further use. (John Gascoine)

Harlow town service 804 commenced operation in 1959 and the basic town service was extended from Bush Fair to Latton Bush in the following year. Here in the town bus station RT602 with duty plates EP32 is seen taking on a respectable load for the short journey to the neighbourhood in the south of the New Town. This RT, here carrying body number 1857, was another which was eventually shipped to Ceylon for further use. (Alan B.Cross)

Ex-RTL1450 had first entered service in March 1953 carrying Park Royal body number 6701. It received an overhaul in June 1956 to be outshopped with an earlier built body number 4447 and was disposed of to Bird's Commercial Motors in August 1959. This was a very short life with the Executive when one considers that the last RT family buses ran in passenger service on 7th April 1979. J.Lloyd & Sons Ltd. of Nuneaton acquired the bus in October 1959 and used it in passenger service until June 1965 when it was involved in an accident which resulted in its premature scrapping. It is seen here in brilliant sunshine, looking immaculate having had a recent repaint. (Alan Mortimer)

RT2060, fitted with body number 2010 since December 1958 when it returned to service from its second overhaul visit to Aldenham, is seen in Brighton on a private hire outing. The sunny weather conditions, wrought iron background familiar in so many Brighton rally photos and temporary police notice evoke memories of years past when such lazily carefree days could be spent at this south coast resort. In April 1964 the RT was disposed of to be exported to the USA and is recorded as having a fairly chequered career before it was finally broken up in July 1980. (Alan Mortimer)

Hounslow garage's trainer bus was RT132 from May 1950 through to July 1962 when it was transferred to Chelverton Road, Putney for further use in the same role. On 8th May it is seen standing on the familiar cobbles of Fulwell depot with its barely concealed tram tracks beneath trolleybus wiring whose last day of usefulness this is. The following day the depot became a garage and it entered its third phase which continues to this day in the ownership of London United Busways. (Ralph E.Stevens)

RF382, having commenced its journey just minutes earlier from the terminus situated behind these buildings, pauses at the front entrance of Uxbridge Station. It is bound for Laleham, the furthest point on the 224 group of routes. The bus dates from December 1952 when it entered service from Old Kent Road garage on Route 202 being one of a batch of six required to replace older Q type buses at this south east London garage. It reached its present garage at Uxbridge immediately after its October 1961 visit to Aldenham for overhaul. (Ron Wellings)

RT34 sustained roof damage late in 1961 when in use as a learner bus and garaged at Chalk Farm. Since last November it has lain within Shepherds Bush garage unlicensed to await its final fate which arrived in November of the year under review with its sale to F.Ridler of London, W11. Quite remarkably, although the roof has been completely decapitated, no distortion in the pillars of the upper deck has taken place which highlights the superb design of the RT body.
(John Gascoine)

Circular town route 802 which visited the town bus station at Stevenage in the course of its ramblings is being worked by RT3504 based at the garage just a short walk away. The London Transport fleet name lacks the London part following half finished accident repair work. Behind, Hatfield's RT3125 works the trunk route 303 to New Barnet Station. Both vehicles were eventually operated by London Country Bus Services Ltd. after the split on 1st January 1970. (Ron Wellings)

Two buses employed on Route 25 have turned short at Aldgate, eschewing the run through the City and West End to Victoria. The lead example RTL1018, complete with driver and running plates BW6, waits to run back east as far as Ilford Broadway while RTL1408 as BW13 parked behind will venture to the normal ultimate destination of Becontree Heath. Both are fitted with Park Royal bodies identical to those originally carried on their Leyland Titan PD2/1 chassis. (Ron Wellings)

RM357 is climbing Bruce Grove, Tottenham on 16th October while in use on the Monday to Saturday Route 243 which had replaced trolleybus services 543 and 643 on 19th July 1961 with the 11th stage of the trolleybus replacement programme. This was a rather restless RM, starting life at Shepherds Bush in 1960 and then moving to Hanwell and Poplar before settling at Stamford Hill in March of the year under review. (John Gascoine)

Originally entering service in Country Area livery from Godstone garage in October 1952, RLH22 was repainted into Central Area red livery at the time of its first overhaul in September 1955. Prior to this date it was already operating from the Central Area Harrow Weald garage to which it returned in its new red paint. Soon after its second overhaul it moved to Dalston where it stayed even after being delicensed to await sale which took place in November 1967, it being one of the large number of the class which found new homes abroad. Here it pounds down the offside lane of Stratford High Street, trafficator flashing for the right hand turn into Carpenters Road. (Alan Mortimer)

The 224A route was double decked with RTs on 9th May and prior to that RF518 waits at Uxbridge Station on the route. The bus, originally RF299, had exchanged its stock number with RF518 in an exercise carried out in 1956 aimed at keeping the various Green Line, Central and Country Area vehicles in their own respective numerical sequences of fleet numbers. RF299 had begun its service within the capital from Muswell Hill garage on Route 210 in September when it was among the first Central Area RFs to commence operation. Through the front nearside window can be seen the doors fitted in April 1959 in readiness for one-man operation but thwarted by Union opposition until 1964. (Alan Mortimer)

GS83 is seen departing from Hemel Hempstead garage on a positioning journey to the bus station for use on Route 316 as HH91. Clearly shown is the latest 'Pay as you enter, Fares ready please' notice now carried on a plate fitted into brackets which had been added to all the vehicles remaining in the class. The fine 1930s architecture of Two Waters garage in the background and the staff car park is now but a memory, the building having been demolished and the land redeveloped. (Alan B.Cross)

Carrying a Saunders built body, RT296 operates from Hounslow garage on the Sunday working of Route 73 over the whole length of the service from Hounslow through to Stoke Newington. On weekdays the route was operated in two sections and the southern part only reached Kensington while the northern arm ventured south as far as Richmond. The bus is seen on the northbound carriageway of Park Lane near to Marble Arch. (Ron Wellings)

RTL164 is resting in Forest Gardens off Bruce Grove, Tottenham before departure to Forest Hill on Route 171. Although two and a half years have passed since its last overhaul it appears to be in reasonable condition. The advertising hoarding refers to the lion mark of quality assured by the Egg Marketing Board at the time while Associated Rediffusion would appear to be counting on the bus staying put for a length of time while you read all the blurb on the side about their Thursday programme at 9.15. (John Gascoine)

An unidentified ex-London Transport Guy Arab exported to Southern Rhodesia in the period 1952/53 still gives yeoman service, albeit with a newer single deck body. Originally having been disposed of to W.North & Sons, dealer of Leeds, it entered passenger service with Trans-Rhodes Services of Salisbury carrying their fleet number 63 with local registration S 34694 and was later rebodied with a South African Blanckenburg single-deck bus body. By 1962 it was operating under the Salisbury United fleet name as their number 1-452 and is seen on 22nd February at their depot in Salisbury. Note the addition of the magnificent manually operated direction indicator arm, guaranteed to knock any cyclist off his bike who passed too close. (L.G.Hooley)

Having arrived at the Biggin Hill Air Display a number of RTs now take a well earned rest in the favourable weather conditions prevailing on 15th September. Nearest the camera RT1000 carries duty plates GD218 for its use on the auxiliary 705 service. The crew have tried to show initiative by displaying the destination Biggin Hill, Black Horse as well as the 'To and From Biggin Hill Air Display' blind. Commendable but anyone wanting the Black Horse would have been left with a little walk! RT3196 behind, although prior to June resident at Godstone, was by now a Chelsham vehicle. (John Gascoine)

Initially disposed of to Bird's Commercial Motors, Stratford upon Avon in April 1960 after a career with London Transport which had lasted from 1st April 1940, RT58 was sold to the Ayrshire Bus Owners' group around September 1961. Sadly being withdrawn in July 1962 it found its way back to Bird's and was eventually reduced to scrap. Seen here leaving the Bus Station in Kilmarnock on 26th May, three further vehicles are left behind: a Western SMT coach registered LCS203, a double deck Leyland with index mark GFN911 and Daimler TCS103. (A.J.Douglas)

After less than a year in passenger service operating in the Country Area from Hatfield garage, green liveried RTL1258 now finds itself demoted to learner duties for much of its remaining time with the Executive. Its trainee driver steers it carefully along Edgware Road while Clapton garage, an RTL stronghold, have wasted no time adding their code to the bus. Its disposal in May 1964 did nothing for the well being of the bus since it was exported to Yugoslavia for further punishment at the hands of its new operators, Gradeka Saobracaine Preduzece of Savajevo. (Alan Mortimer)

RT4174 is about to turn off Station Road at Kings Langley into the main gates of the Ovaltine Works to position itself for a return journey to Bushey Station on Route 301A. The occupants of the Vauxhall Viva probably cannot understand why they should be the subjects of a photograph while the Danger sign for eager home going workers is strategically placed on the far side of the rather narrow unclassified road. (Alan B.Cross)

RT655 is seen in Baker Street having just crossed the junction with Marylebone Road on its journey to London Bridge as duty RL27. First entering service in the summer of 1948 the vehicle lasted in passenger use for another three years before being disposed of for scrap to C.Hoyle & Sons Ltd. of Wombwell in July 1965. (Alan Mortimer)

Well laden RT2508 circumnavigates a roundabout as it journeys from Harlow Mill Station to Potter Street via Brays Grove situated to the south of the town. This fleet number first appeared in February 1950 when the chassis carried a Weymann built body but before its eventual sale in March 1971 it had gone through several body changes. (Alan B.Cross)

RFW10, while engaged on City Tour duties, has called into the Minories bus and coach station at Aldgate. The driver appears to be opening his windscreen indicating warm weather to accompany the bright sunshine. Towards the end of the following year this example from the fifteen strong class was withdrawn from use together with ten others. In early 1965 it was exported to Ceylon, being one of ten which found further use with Transboard Tours, the touring arm of the Ceylon Transport Board. (Tom Smith)

RM1132 takes passengers on board in Kingston Road at New Malden. The trolleybus wiring is in the process of being dismantled although the poles look likely to remain since they are serving a useful function as lampposts and in this case as a bus stop post. The 285 route was a rather more lengthy replacement for the 605 trolleybus. It came from Haydons Road Station beyond Wimbledon and went right into London Airport Central. The Heathrow name was yet to become common usage. (Alan B.Cross)

Watford town centre finds RT611 in use on Route 318 to Sarratt. This RT was one of the Country Area batch originally carrying RT3 type bodywork with a roof box. It now carries body number 7261 of RT8 classification which no doubt helped ensure its longevity for it was finally sold for scrap to Wombwell Diesels in April 1977. (A.B.Cross)

It was on 20th May of the year under review that the first rumblings of the now massive one-way system in Watford began. Here in January RF581 unloads its passengers in Watford High Street facing north. Clements department store sign is just visible above the bus which helps place the picture in the modern context. Now the Exchange Road flyover crosses here over a pedestrianised area. The 319 route from Chipperfield was unique in its destination, 'Watford, Clarendon Corner'. The passengers are alighting a little north of that point and when the section of the High Street south of Clarendon Corner was pedestrianised on 20th May the terminal description changed to 'Watford, Parade' although ostensibly it was the same point. Nowadays the 319, operated by Red Rose, still serves Chipperfield, Kings and Abbots Langley but only one return journey reaches Watford and that comes from the Chipperfield end of the route rather than Abbots Langley as this bus has done. (Ron Wellings)

RM1269 stands just inside Finchley garage awaiting Union negotiations, having been delivered to the Executive in June. Eventually it entered service at Mortlake garage in December as part of the package to convert Route 73 to the new type of vehicle. No route blinds or garage codes are carried since when delivered the management hoped that EW or HD codes would be required but this was not to be.

RMC1460 entered service operating from Guildford garage in August. A few days into its career with London Transport it is seen at Brook Green in Shepherds Bush Road en-route for Hertford. As delivered these coaches carried the cast metal Green Line motif midway along the length of the body between decks with the relief colour broken in the area of the air intake grille for the heating and ventilating system. Double headlights either side of the radiator grille, revised front blind apertures and platform doors were fitted for their Green Line duties.
(J.G.S.Smith collection)

Two Crawley garaged RTs in the shape of RT3044 nearest the camera and RT3456 beyond, stand in Crawley bus station both destined for Rutherford Way. The 405B route had been introduced on 25th October of the previous year replacing the 476B and some journeys on the 405. The 853A service had previously served Gatwick Airport but was cut back to Rutherford Way on 17th January of the year under review. (A.B.Cross)

It was during June that GS39 was transferred to East Grinstead garage from its previous home of Amersham although its stay at this West Sussex outpost was short-lived. In February 1963 it was again on the move, this time to Dorking where it resided for the remainder of its passenger use. Commencing its journey out of East Grinstead on Route 494 a leisurely trip to Oxted Station is ensured on a route which was involved with this class of bus from December 1953 through to 6th May 1964 when one man operated RFs were introduced as replacements.

Journeying only as far as West Molesey, Norbiton's RT686 was photographed on Route 131 on 8th May, the day before major changes were made to the route in connection with the final stage of trolleybus conversion. This RT would be replaced by a sparkling new RM and consigned to store at Camberwell garage until November when it would be put back into service from Alperton. (Ray Stanmore)

Finchley garage's RM910 first entered service in November 1961 when motorbus route 221 replaced the 521/621 trolleybuses. Now eleven months later on 10th October the bus waits amid the office blocks of the Farringdon Street terminus. This rear view shows the rear blind layout and use of the offside route blind practiced in 1962. (Alan B.Cross)

RT820 managed to lose this roof mounted route number box body at its November 1964 overhaul which was to ensure the longevity of the fleet number. It is seen at Gants Hill operating on Route 144 from Leyton garage which first became involved with the route in November 1940 and was to remain the main supplier of vehicles until 1964. (Ron Wellings)

An interesting shot inside Shepherds Bush garage taken on 14th April reveals RM432, which suffered lower rear end damage earlier in the month, awaiting repair. It had been in service since November 1960 when it took to the road from Hanwell garage arriving at its present home in March 1961. RM1161 and RM1162 have been stored since being handed over to the Executive and are awaiting entry into service from Stonebridge Park garage in May replacing vehicles which had first operated from that garage on 3rd January and which were passed on to Fulwell and Hounslow at the final stage of the trolleybus conversions. (Roger Partridge)

This scene of the bridge rebuilding and road lowering and widening scheme at Worcester Park station will also interest railway enthusiasts. On 28th October RF369 journeys to Belmont station having commenced its service at Kingston bus station. It had been transferred to Kingston garage in January 1962 and was to reside here until the time of its third visit to Aldenham for overhaul in January 1965 when it was adapted for one man operation, re-entering service at Edgware. As a temporary measure Route 213 was split in two at this location while work was carried out on the bridge span on 4th November. Note the temporary sign pointing to the station footbridge and also the new railway bridge retaining structure already in place as can be seen beneath the driver's cab of the electric multiple unit. (H.E.Murrell)

Route 106A was a Sunday variant of the weekday 106 which deviated off the main Becontree route through Rippleside to Dagenham. RTL1241 passes through 'the Narrow' as locals call this section of Mare Street, Hackney on 10th June with the greater part of the route still to be covered before New Road at Dagenham is reached. At one time Sunday extensions of routes ran that way to the 'Ship and Shovel' at Rippleside offering Eastenders a breath of fresh air but 1962 Dagenham was hardly that! In February 1968 Waldens Coaches of Epping became the new owner of this RTL which was then just over sixteen years of age. (John Gascoine)

RMs 1214, 1215, 1201, 1212, 1058 and 1213 are seen at the Park Royal works on 23rd April awaiting movement to the Executive. RM1058 obviously had some defect since it had remained at Aldenham since delivery in December 1961 and was now back at the body builders. It eventually entered service from Fulwell in May. Of the others, RM1212 was in passenger use from Hounslow during May but the rest, after storage at Edmonton garage, were not to enter service until December. (Roger Partridge)

On the first day of Tottenham RM operation on Route 73 the eleven AEC engined examples in their allocation were not the only such buses to be put on the road from this garage whose double deck fleet had previously been all Leyland. At Stoke Newington RT3755, on loan from Wood Green, is seen on duty AR35 about to depart for Hammersmith Broadway. Obviously there was some upheaval on 12th December since the RTL just visible behind has its destination display set for Goodge Street Station, a definitely unscheduled turn. (John Gascoine)

On its journey to far off Dorking on Route 470 RT1097 traverses Station Road at West Croydon. This bus is one of Chelsham garage's contribution to the route which was also shared with buses and crews from Leatherhead. A Ford car with white wall tyres, which were all the rage in the United States but which thankfully never really took off on this side of the Atlantic, follows closely behind. Note the bus stop zone plate W11 above the familiar compulsory flag. This system had been introduced here in 1961. (Ron Wellings)

Route 332 was a new GS operated service introduced in January 1958, primarily for school children and operated between Amersham garage and Quill Hall Estate. GS64 departs the garage with at least three older passengers. On 24th October of the year under review the entire GS operation at this garage, which had witnessed the largest concentration of the class, was replaced by one man operated RF type buses, sadly depriving the local populace of the distinctive sound of these Perkins engined vehicles. This particular bus, although withdrawn from service in May 1967 was nevertheless transferred to London Country Bus Services Ltd. upon its formation on 1st January 1970. It was sold to Tillingbourne Valley Services Ltd. in April 1971 and after a chequered career is currently held in the reserve fleet of the London Transport Museum. (A.B.Cross)

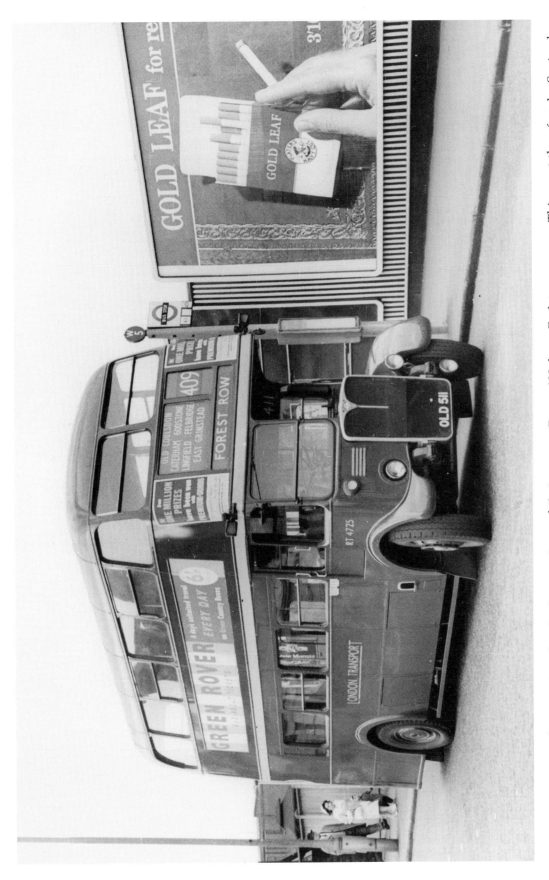

RT4725 lays over at the West Croydon Station terminus while in use on Route 409 from Godstone garage. This must therefore be September since this was the one month it operated from GD. Following its overhaul in June, when it was outshopped with body number 9003, it spent one month at East Grinstead followed by a similar period at Garston before coming to Godstone in September. Transferred to Dorking in October and Amersham in November before its next move in January of the following year, it is obvious there must be a reason for such a footloose existence. All becomes clear when you realise the bus was fitted with a loadmaster device for measuring the number of passengers carried. General rather than local advertisements are carried - a day's unlimited travel on Green Country buses then cost 6/- (30p) and the front of the bus tells us that over one million prizes have been won with Premium Bonds - I wonder what the figure is now? (Ron Wellings)

On 13th April at the 'King's Arms' RTL1567 working from Walworth garage crosses Peckham Rye on its way to Westminster while a fellow 184 passes in the other direction towards Brockley Station. In the distance can be seen the clock tower of the former Nunhead garage, at this time leased to Charles W.Banfield for coach operation. The two types of 'Keep Left' bollards are interesting, the older example still in situ awaiting replacement by the newer utilitarian design. (Roger Partridge)

RT150 finished its passenger carrying service in June 1955 when transferred from Chelverton Road, Putney to storage at Stockwell garage. It soon re-appeared on the roads of the capital as a staff bus, being garaged initially at New Cross and later at Twickenham. In October 1959 it commenced a further phase of its life as a learner vehicle and it is seen fulfilling this role while garaged at Hounslow. The end of London Transport ownership arrived in June 1963 when it was disposed of to F.Ridler of London W11 still carrying body number 428 with which it had entered service in June 1941. (Photomatic Ltd.)

RF483 climbs Wimbledon Hill Road where at the summit it will turn left into Ridgway leaving the following bus on Route 93 to continue its journey towards Putney. In service with a two man crew the RF would eventually be converted to one man operation in June 1965 but for now passengers have the added luxury of a not exactly overworked conductor. On the other side of the road a lady sits at the spot where, on 2nd January 1951 in atrocious weather conditions, Putney Bridge garaged RT22 toppled over on to its side never to re-enter service again. (Alan Mortimer)

Quite a number of passengers have availed themselves of a seat within Saunders bodied RT1329 while it waits to commence another run as AV1 from the terminus at Hounslow Garage. The 110 route still provides the same journey to Twickenham via Powder Mill Lane but you will note that the blind provides for the peak hour extension from Hounslow to Cranford which operated in 1962. The bus, having received an overhaul at Aldenham in April, looks in pristine condition in this view taken on 7th September. (Tom Smith)

RT1076 is caught at North Watford in service on Route 346E, a school special which connected St.Michael's School with Carpenders Park Station. The pupils all appear to be seated, a bit of a rarity on a school bus nowadays, and most are in conversation though at least two have spotted the photographer and are temporarily distracted. After a career with London Transport the bus moved on for further use with London Country Bus Services Ltd. being withdrawn in March 1972 and sold for scrap. (A.B.Cross)

Route number 247A was in use from December 1950 through to September 1982 when the service was renumbered plain 247. Here RT1705, a resident of North Street, Romford since November 1957, is about to depart from the bus stop in South Street, Romford to continue its journey to Harold Hill. After further use with other operators it moved into the preservation movement in the early 70s and nowadays it regularly attends various rallies during the season. (Alan Mortimer)

GS33 leaves Tring garage on a short journey to the nearby village of Wigginton. The turn at that village was made by a reverse manoeuvre on the Chesham Road into Lower Wigginton at Wigginton Bottom. The 397 route was more usually associated with Amersham garage but this local working is with a Tring vehicle. (Ron Wellings)

RTL1516 emerges from Tottenham garage for the last time as it departs on its transfer journey to Stockwell. The date is 12th December and interestingly although the garage was built in 1913, adequate headroom for modern vehicles was provided. The smooth oblong concrete expanse between the two portals once held the inscription 'The Tramways, 19(MET)13, Omnibus Co.Ltd.' and this, together with addition of various notices and lighting, is the only cosmetic change to have been made to the frontage of the building up to 1962. In latter years however the facade has been modernised. (John Gascoine)

During December of the previous year the RW class of three buses moved en-bloc to St.Albans garage for use on Route 355. Having just left the terminus at Church Green, Harpenden RW1 is working the additional service provided from there to Batford Estate, Pickford Hill as the route blind shows. (Alan Mortimer)

Standing inside West Ham garage on 9th June the first buses in the two lines represent twenty years development in the design and construction of the London double deck bus. RT10 beside the wall was taken into stock in February 1940 to enter service on 1st May from Chelverton Road, Putney garage. It has served as a training vehicle for many years now and in May of the following year it will be disposed of. RM41 on the other hand was delivered in August 1959 to enter service later in the month from Cricklewood garage for evaluation purposes on Route 2. At the time the RT, which now carries the body previously on RT68, was sold to its new owner the Barking Metal Trading Company, RM41 had just received its first overhaul being outshopped with the body first fitted to RM18. (John Gascoine)

Merton garage had received RT2390, now fitted with a Saunders built body number 2529, immediately after its 1960 overhaul. In use on Route 152 it is seen standing at the Feltham Station terminus about to depart on its journey to 'The Cricketers' at Mitcham in dry January weather. One small schoolboy has availed himself of the popular lower deck front seat with at least one other passenger to keep him company. (Ron Wellings)

RT350 spent its last year of passenger service within the capital garaged at Bromley. On 17th April it is seen traversing Pickhurst Lane nearing the end of the weekday route 138 to Coney Hall. Arlington Motors of Ponders End, who were not normally associated with the disposal of the class, took twelve in April 1963 and this example passed on to Lloyd of Nuneaton in the following month. (Roger Partridge)

Working as HD1 on 1st May, this Weymann bodied lowbridge RLH70 had reached its current place of residence after its return to service from its October 1956 overhaul. Previously Merton garage had operated the bus since new in December 1952 basically on their lowbridge route 127. Route 230 running between the two points carried on the blind was renumbered H1 in June 1969 and lasted through to November 1987 when it was withdrawn. Soon after the route was revamped in 1969 this bus left these shores for another life in the U.S.A. (Tom Smith)

The date is 14th April and RF379 waits at Hounslow Bus Station for its next journey on Route 237 to Chertsey Station as AV3. The slipboard carried advises that there is a minimum fare in operation over part of the route while the British Rail 'go by train mid-week' advertisement degrades the overall appearance of the pleasing lines of the Metro-Cammell body. The route number can be traced back to the large renumbering exercise of 3rd October 1934 when the DA operated 137 route became 237. (Roger Partridge)

Potters Bar garage was to be the last operational base for RT334 which had only had two previous allocations: Upton Park and Bromley. During this time it had received four overhauls and on the last occasion in July 1958 it was outshopped with body number 1438 which originally graced the chassis of RT189. A recent fall of snow on 2nd January is in evidence as the bus turns off Hampstead Road. Doubtless the weather conditions account for its unusual short working to Charing Cross.
(Alan Mortimer)

With Grays garage not too far away the lead bus, RT646, carries a side blind to the front which makes doubly sure that passengers know it is working Route 328A which operated between Bulphan and Purfleet Station, although here it is only working the western section with appropriate blind. Three further garages would use this roof boxed bus carrying body number 1870 before it was disposed of in May 1964. RT4206 following and about to overtake is in use on Route 328 and is also terminating short at Grays. (Ron Wellings)

Route number 260 was resurrected with the thirteenth stage of the trolleybus conversion programme which took place on 3rd January. It had last been used for a service between Colindale and Surrey Docks which was renumbered 60 in October of the previous year. Now it was used as a replacement for trolleybus service 660 with a northerly extension to Barnet previously covered by the 645 route. RM type buses from Finchley and Stonebridge garages were the normal vehicles to be found on the route but on Sundays Cricklewood provided five RTs. As duty W4, Park Royal bodied RT4797 is seen operating as far as Harlesden which was the southern terminus on Sunday and although Cricklewood buses never worked beyond to Hammersmith the intermediate point blind provided covered that section. (Alan Mortimer)

With buildings which show signs of having changed owners as a background, RM839 approaches Shoreditch on the Sunday only Route 243A which ran to London Docks, Leman Street from the northern terminus of Wood Green. Celebrating its first year of service to Londoners while being garaged at Stamford Hill, this RM was to be transferred to West Ham in April 1963. (Ron Wellings)

RF430 is seen turning off the main A113 on to the B172 road at Abridge to continue its journey through Theydon Bois and Ivy Chimneys to Epping. Route 250 had all the air of a country area bus service and yet had always been a Central Area route. By 1962 it was operated by North Street, Romford garage, having formerly worked from Hornchurch which was still its southern terminus. The route originated with Capitol Road Transport Ltd. in September 1929 as far as Abridge, reaching Epping in 1930. It became LGOC G7 in 1932 and LPTB 250 in 1934. Nowadays Route 500 follows similar roads from Romford venturing northward beyond Epping to Harlow and Stansted Airport and is worked on weekdays by County Bus and Thamesway on Sundays. (Alan Mortimer)

Route number 4A had previously been in use for a weekday service operating between Finsbury Park and Clapham Common, being withdrawn in August 1958. On 8th November 1961 it returned to the Finsbury Park to St.Pauls section of road as a Monday to Friday service operating between Finsbury Park and Waterloo, cut back to Aldwych in the evenings. RT3561 is seen at Waterloo departing for a journey back to Holloway garage which was its home base. Other buses in view are operating on routes 46 and 199 while another 4A vehicle completes the picture. This is now the site of the Red Arrow garage. (Ron Wellings)

RF451 fitted with body number 7930 spent the period from August 1961 through to August 1965 garaged at Tottenham. It is seen here on the garage's only single deck route, the number 236, on which it shared operation with Leyton. In rainy conditions it crosses Seven Sisters Road at Finsbury Park Station on 21st April typically lacking a route number stencil above the saloon entrance. (Roger Partridge)

The Biggin Hill Air Display always attracted considerable numbers of air enthusiasts, many of which made the journey by special excursions. To the extreme left of this array on 15th September is Godstone garaged RF278 while the three double deckers are RT4239, RT1878 and RT3728. The first two are red liveried and on loan to Dartford garage while RT3728 in Country Area colours has made the journey from Northfleet garage having picked up its passengers at Gravesend. (John Gascoine)

RT2390 had re-entered service from its September 1961 overhaul carrying a Saunders RT3/3 body numbered 2529 having originally been fitted with a Weymann RT8/2 example when new in December 1949. The main arterial A3 road at Shannon Corner begins to show the increasing number of private motor cars. The Decca flag flies proudly over their factory which overlooks an interchange which has now altered beyond all recognition. (Ron Wellings)

When photographed on 1st July in Clifton Terrace, Finsbury Park RF324 was a long way from its normal haunts plying for custom on Route 211 between Ealing Broadway and Greenford while garaged at Southall. Note the Milletts advertisement on the cantrail complete with an Ealing telephone number which is rather inappropriate for the passers by on the course of Route 210 between Finsbury Park and Golders Green. Only temporarily on loan, it was returned to HW in due course where it was to remain until its July 1964 visit to Aldenham for overhaul. (John Gascoine)

Confined to the eastern section during the week, Route 107A from Enfield Lock ventured beyond Enfield Chase and Oakwood on a Sunday to Edgware Station. Enfield's RT2882 pulls away from the traffic lights in Hertford Road to turn right into Southbury Road at Ponders End with a respectable loading. The Triumph car driver's attention is momentarily distracted by the photographer and perhaps his passenger is telling him to look where he is going. (Ron Wellings)

Peckham garaged RT1344 stands in Claremont Road, West Kilburn, the northern terminus of Route 36. This route ran from here to Hither Green Station from June 1914 right through until April 1991 when traffic congestion meant its southern section between Lewisham and Hither Green was entrusted to the more localised 180 route, although even that has now been superseded. The conductress enjoys a few minutes conversation with her somewhat older looking driver, while the inevitable Gibson ticket machine is suspended from her shoulders. (Ron Wellings)

RF127 nears the end of its journey into central London from Hertford as it passes Little Portland Street approaching Oxford Circus. A graphic reminder of the ever changing political scene throughout the world is provided by the USSR tourist offices situated on the corner with Regent Street. The 715A was always a poor relation of the busy 715 Hertford - Guildford route and between Waltham Cross and Manor House ran via Ponders End, Edmonton and Tottenham instead of Enfield, Palmers Green and Wood Green. It lasted from 1956 to 1969 with the single deck RFs being replaced by RMCs on 29th August of the year under review. However, such was its underuse that by the time of its withdrawal the RFs had returned. (Ron Wellings)

Red liveried RF506 on loan to Reigate garage from February through to October easily passes under the 12'6" headroom of the railway bridge at Salfords. Having just commenced a journey on Route 440 from the Monotype Works, a right hand turn on to the A23 main trunk road will suffice for the bus to reach its destination at Redhill some two miles distant. (Alan Mortimer)

This photograph taken inside Poplar garage on 9th June shows RM318 unlicensed and stored with RTL1036 resting from its duties on Route 82. The excellent series of 'TLB Extra' publications produced by LOTS confirms that between May and October the RM was off the road. The RTL had been transferred from nearby Athol Street garage during June 1958 and was to reside here at Poplar until its third visit to works for overhaul. (John Gascoine)

The bus terminus incorporated into the roundabout at Muswell Hill Broadway is amazingly still in use to this day but unfortunately does not accommodate the once ubiquitous RT. Park Royal bodied RT241 saw out its final years of passenger service with London Transport at Muswell Hill garage to be finally delicensed and put in store at Edmonton to await its disposal. Route 212 had been converted to double deck operation in January 1960 when the weak bridge over the railway at the former Muswell Hill Station had been eradicated. The route was renumbered W7 in May 1969 when single deck vehicles returned for a while and is nowadays operated by MTL. (W.R.Legg)

RT3666 presently operates from Grays garage which was only its third and as it was to turn out last, having previously seen service from Chelsham and Leatherhead since it was new in February 1953, being disposed of by the Executive in December 1963. It is seen in service journeying to Stifford Clays by way of Route 323B. The 323 group of routes all used Purfleet as their western terminus, passing through Grays to their different destinations of Woodside Estate (323), Nutberry Corner (323A) and Stifford Clays (323B). (Ron Wellings)

Seen in Plimsoll Road, Finsbury Park on 1st July are RF337 with RTL928 parked somewhat erratically behind. The RF is soon to depart from its resting place on its back street run to Leyton High Road, Hainault Road as duty T3 on the 236 route. Tooting Bec Station is to be the next destination of the Battersea garaged RTL on Route 19 but for the moment doubtless both crews are in the staff canteen alongside the terminus. (John Gascoine)

This picture of RT1616 on Route 406 makes an interesting comparison with that of ST894 which appeared on page 89 of the 1948 book of this series. Amazingly both buses are parked in the identical position at Kingston Station with their front offside wheel just beside the same white painted kerbstone. All the buildings in the background remain intact with the inscribed concrete plaque 'Built by A.Cowen 1932' still on view. The only change of significance is the brick perimeter wall which has replaced the chestnut paling fence. (Alan Mortimer)

EX-RTL15, now in service with Central SMT carries their fleet number HL192 having previously been operated by J.Laurie who traded as Chieftain bearing their number 54. It was only a short while into service with its newest owner when it was involved in an accident which necessitated the front end being rebuilt. This included the top deck windows, now of the non-opening variety and rebuilt cab. The opportunity was taken to incorporate standard Central SMT blind boxes. The rear view mirrors look decidedly of inferior quality to those worn in earlier years. A nice array of Bristols together with a further Leyland keep this Leyland 7RT bus company in this view taken on 22nd September at Motherwell. (A.J.Douglas)

T790, with only a few months further use in passenger service left before withdrawal in June, was to become the penultimate vehicle of a class which had served Londoners continuously since 1929. It is seen standing on the upward slope from Tring garage with handbrake fully on before departure as far as the station on the Tring town route 387 working duty TG2. Having first passed through the hands of L.W.Vass, the dealer of Ampthill it was acquired by Bovis the well established house builder in March 1963. Nothing further is recorded after further sale to Smith, a dealer of Leighton Buzzard in 1967. (Ron Wellings)

GS83 is seen in the Hemel Hempstead bus station early in the year as passengers board the little 26 seater for a journey which will take the bus to Chesham Broadway. Eighteen of this class were withdrawn from service in October being the largest number to be taken out of passenger use in any one month and this example was included. Having first entered service in December 1954 operating from Crawley garage after spending nearly a year in store, a similar fate was to befall it after its final use at Hemel Hempstead. Eventually it was sold to the British Railways Board (Midland Region) in November 1963 and used to transport students to and from their Work Study Training Centre at Watford. It is not one of the thirty or so known to be preserved but was sold for scrap in 1967. (Ron Wellings)

Two former Craven bodied RTs are captured for good measure in this scene as they run through Saltcoats on 1st July. Both vehicles are part of the Ayrshire Bus Owners' fleet, the lead bus, ex-RT1496 now fleet number 43, being owned by Hunter of Kilmarnock and ex-RT1403 of Hill and Patterson follows behind. Both are bound for Ardrossan but via different routes, the details of which are hard to read being crammed into the destination box. It is strange how in the main operators of ex-London vehicles failed to use the equipment they had acquired properly. (A.J.Douglas)

All the variants of the 377 group of works services passed through the amusingly named Cupid Green on the northern fringes of Hemel Hempstead. This 377B seen on the A41 is terminating there rather than continuing to Friars Wash. RT4562, which originally operated in red livery from Sutton and Leyton garages, received Country Area colours at its June 1961 overhaul. It only saw service use at Hemel Hempstead and St.Albans before visiting Aldenham works in December 1965 once again returning to its old red livery. (Alan B.Cross)

Hertford bus station in the late autumn witnesses RW1 and RW2 in use on two of the routes they were involved with after their transfer to Hertford garage during September. This garage evaluated these buses on a greater variety of routes than any other had done previously and they could be found on the 331, 333, 333B, 384 and 390 at sometime during their short stay. RW2 nearest the camera as duty HG47 waits to depart on a journey on 390 to Stevenage Station mainly on the A602 while RW1 will head up the line of the Roman Ermine Street from Ware more commonly known as the A10 trunk road to reach its Route 331 destination of Buntingford. (Ron Wellings)

Watford cross town route 346 linked the Oxhey Estate in the south with Kingswood in the north and Garston garaged RT2121 journeys to Hallowes Crescent, its southern terminus. Originally the bus had entered service in January 1950 operating from Holloway garage, being one of six new chassis on to which second hand surplus bodies from the float system were mounted. The resulting hybrid meant new chassis number 09613390 carried body 1540, which for some reason had been removed prematurely from the chassis of RT291. Since receiving green livery upon its July 1956 overhaul, a further visit to Aldenham now sees the bus carrying body number 2245 and in this form it would be disposed of in May of the following year for further service in Ceylon. (A.B.Cross)

In the early hours of the morning, long before the rush hour traffic and the tourists fill up the empty spaces, TD95 on staff bus duties picks up Underground workers at Piccadilly Circus. Being garaged at Edgware, daytime work on Route 240A will probably be the humdrum task afforded the bus and this venture into the central area of the capital will provide the vehicle with some respite from the monotony. (Alan Mortimer)

Once the trolleybus conversion programme had finished some hard negotiations had to take place with the Unions before the conversion of routes from RT family buses to the new RM type could begin. Eventually succumbing to a one for one replacement programme, Route 73 was one of the first to be converted. On 12th December, the first day of use, RM1301 is seen parked at Stoke Newington to begin its long career serving Londoners. Just why the rear destination blind is showing Edmonton, Tramway Avenue is a mystery. This bus hadn't even been stored there, spending its first four months in store at Walthamstow. (John Gascoine)

This view taken at Edgware Station bus terminus clearly shows the basic two differing types of blind box layouts fitted to the RT family of vehicles. Nearest to the camera RT372 carries a Park Royal built RT3 coded body numbered 2033 and originally fitted to RT754. RT684 to the left of the picture had entered service in June 1948 with a roof route number box body but now carries Weymann body number 6225 built in 1951 by which time the three apertures were again carried in between decks as they had been on earlier STLs. RT372 was disposed of in April 1964 while RT684 soldiered on until August 1977 solely as a result of the type of body carried at a particular time. (Ron Wellings)

RF618 turns into Clarendon Road from Woodford Road at Watford Junction as it starts its journey to Hemel Hempstead, Highfield on Route 322. The bus, although bearing a certain amount of dust, still gleams from its May overhaul. In January of the following year it was trasnferred to St.Albans with a further move eastwards to Hertford garage, its home prior to its visit to Aldenham. Of interest is the prominent advertising for coal, the quality, comfort and economy fuel that coal merchants Wallace Spiers & Co.Ltd., whose office occupies part of the present bus station/car park, can deliver with a call into their order office. Oil and gas fired central heating had not yet become the norm. (Alan Mortimer)

Once G423 in the London Transport fleet this Guy Arab II with Weymann bodywork had first entered service in December 1945. Disposed of in November 1951 to the Scottish Omnibus Group it was assigned to associated company W.Alexander & Sons of Falkirk as fleet number RO639 during the same month. With decentralization of the Alexander business in 1961 the bus along with six others moved into the newly formed W.Alexander & Sons (Fife) Ltd. Now carrying the Cowdenbeath (C) garage code plate fixed to the cab air vent, it is seen in Kirkcaldy on 24th September waiting to depart for Lochgelly on the 334 service just weeks before being withdrawn from passenger service. All seven former London Guy Arabs which had been operated were taken out of service before the end of the year and disposed of to dealers for scrap. (A.J.Douglas)

The passengers seated within RF18 at Aldgate on 21st April will not realise that in June the coach would be withdrawn from London Transport. It was in May 1951 that Streatham garage had had the honour of housing this then private hire coach finished in an attractive green and grey livery with red fleet names and numbers. In 1956 the batch RF16 - 25 were repainted into Green Line livery but retained their cantrail roof windows. Being the very first of the 700 strong class to be withdrawn further use was assured for this vehicle and in later years it could be seen in use with the Erne Bus Service of Carrigallon with the Irish registration number IT6226. (Roger Partridge)

RT770 operating from Abbey Wood garage has just commenced service on Route 161 from Woolwich to Chislehurst, War Memorial. This route had provided the service between Eltham and Chislehurst since 1938 and from 1941 had an express peak hour working on from Eltham to Woolwich. This became a normal all day service with the tram conversion of July 1952 and Abbey Wood maintained the tradition of working the road to Eltham although no longer with tramcars. (Ron Wellings)

Parked within the grounds of Cricklewood garage on 14th April, ex-RT106, which has carried service vehicle fleet number 1036TV since December 1955 in connection with its use as a turnover demonstration unit, looks just too pitiful for words. Many windows have been replaced with metal panels while the bodywork has had lifting holes inserted to both sides of the upper deck. It occurs to me that a real bus which has turned over wouldn't have such convenient apertures! This service vehicle was eventually disposed of in March 1971 to end London Transport's involvement with the 2RT2 class which had commenced in 1939. (Roger Partridge)

Heading towards town on Barnet Road at Potters Bar, RT3359 in service on Route 134 sets out on another long journey from Potters Bar to Pimlico, a nicely alliterative set of termini. The operational life span of this RT with London Transport stretched from November 1951 when it entered service at Cricklewood through to July 1964 when it was delicensed at Potters Bar to await disposal. Originally fitted with a Weymann body, number 7196, it is now seen carrying a Park Royal example numbered 1932. For a brief period in 1977 it was in the ownership of preservationists but unfortunateley after being damaged by vandals had to be scrapped. (Alan Mortimer)

Inside Clapton garage on 10th February RTL980 and RTL482 take their rest from their labours on Route 170. Both carry Hackney Station destinations which was the usual one for buses terminating at the garage. However, the nearer bus has a via point blind for the full length of the route from Leyton to Wandsworth while the further bus has the special display which in 1962 was used for early Sunday morning journeys between Leyton and Bloomsbury. (John Gascoine)

With the work in progress on the massive alterations to the road system at Hyde Park Corner RF255 makes a fine picture while working the long 707 route from Oxted to Aylesbury. The sticker placed in the second saloon window announces that the Oval cricket ground is near to the roads served by the coach. After a lengthy career ending as a bus in August 1975, it was withdrawn by London Country Bus Services to enter a new era mainly in the preservation movement, notably providing a vintage service for Metrobus Route 746 in later years. (Alan Mortimer)

RT4761 sets out from High Wycombe garage in early spring sunshine for the slog up to Widmer End on one of the few journeys left on Route 366. The route number was to disappear from the High Wycombe area on 20th June being replaced by journeys on Route 362A which already served Widmer End. (Ron Wellings)

The slipboard carried by RT3323 in use on the Express service of Route 292 reads 'Stopping at all stops in Borehamwood to Stirling Cnr. then Burnt Oak Station'. Despite appearances this is not a steam powered bus! Route 292 operating on a Monday to Saturday basis had been introduced with the 13th stage of the trolleybus conversion programme on 3rd January and it replaced the 52A including the similar express service on this route. Edgware garage provided the vehicles in the form of RTs which operated from the developing Borehamwood area to Colindale on Saturdays being extended to Willesden garage on Mondays to Fridays. This is the Annesley Avenue stand at Colindale which was only served on weekdays, the Sunday service to Borehamwood being provided by the 52 from Victoria. (Ron Wellings)

Since re-entering service from its November 1961 overhaul, RF362 has been garaged at Kingston and on 6th May it is heading home on Portsmouth Road. A trolleybus on service 602 follows which has just left the Dittons terminus but will take the more circuitous route through Surbiton into Kingston. It is just three days before the trolleybus would no longer ply for passengers within the capital, the 602 service being replaced initially by motorbus Route 282, whereas Route 218, which operated between Kingston and Staines, would eventually be taken over by London Country South West in October 1986. (John Gascoine)

This particular use of the route number 44 can be traced back to the first stage of the post war tram conversion programme which took place on 1st October 1950. The route replaced the trolleybus service 612 and tram service 12. Nowadays its two termini are restricted to Tooting Station and Vauxhall and buses in the livery of London General ply the route. Here on 31st October, RTL598 waits at London Bridge Station with crew resting in the lower saloon until time for departure beyond Tooting to Mitcham, The Cricketers. (John Gascoine)

The familiar light coloured stone faced war memorial at Golders Green stands out against the red brick built shops and flats in this view which includes RTL70 soon to depart for Crystal Palace on Route 2. The 'clippie' appears to be in conversation with an inspector and her driver just visible through the lower saloon windows. It would also appear that a person or persons unknown have appropriated the radiator badge from this Leyland PD2/1. Although this long standing route was withdrawn in October 1992 it was resurrected within the year and still plies between Marylebone and Crystal Palace. (W.R.Legg)

From 3rd January, with the closure of West Green garage, Route 233 utilised RT type buses from Wood Green. The familiar sound of the Leyland engined RTL buses previously used was now but a memory. RT1848 was a newcomer to WN garage having been transferred in from West Ham together with a large number of its sisters when the vast majority of West Green's allocation of RTLs took over operations at WH which had previously only held RM or RT buses. This RT did not spend a sustained period of use at its new home as in July 1963 it was delicensed to await disposal which occurred in January 1964 with its sale to a French organisation. (Alan Mortimer)

High Wycombe garaged RT3203 heads round Shepherds Bush Green with much recreational activity taking place on what Terry Wogan once called the rural meadow of Shepherds Bush Common. The bus was overhauled in August of the year under review and seems to be carrying a very good load of passengers on this Green Line relief duty. (A.B.Cross)

Anderson Brothers, trading as Blue Belle of Evenwood, had acquired ex-RTL18 and RTL276 in August 1959 via Bird's the dealer of Stratford-upon-Avon. The business was acquired by O.K.Motor Services Ltd. of Bishops Auckland in January 1960 and these two vehicles were added to a fleet which already included a number of the type. Looking smart in their new owner's colour scheme they were to give many years further service before eventually being disposed of for scrapping. (Alan Mortimer)

Parked under the familiar chestnut trees at Hampton Court on 8th May, private hire RFW12 stands deserted in brilliant sunshine. These eight feet wide and thirty feet long ECW bodied AEC Regal IVs were regarded as the height of luxury, especially for long distance journeys, when they were delivered during the early summer months of 1951. The custodian of this coach, Riverside garage, did not feature prominently in the allocation of these vehicles but was the last operational base for this particular example. (David Berwick)

RTL134 stands in Regents Avenue outside Palmers Green garage at the terminal stand for Route 112. Now fitted with the body of a much higher numbered member of the class it shows some wear mid-way between overhauls. Stonebridge Park garage replaced the Cricklewood and Willesden allocations on Route 112 on 3rd January, which was the day they converted from trolleybus to motorbus. For this purpose they received a small fleet of RTLs and their gleaming new Routemasters did not appear on the North Circular Road service until 1970 and then only on Sundays. (Michael Rooum)

This is ex-RTL30 another of the fifteen members of the class which were taken over by Central SMT from the business of J.Laurie & Co., Burnbank, Hamilton on 1st October 1961. As with RTL12 shown earlier in this book, the previous operator's fleet name and livery is still carried but it has received its new owner's fleet number. It was January 1958 when this Park Royal bodied Leyland Titan found itself one of the first six of the class to be disposed of by London Transport to the dealer, Bird's Commercial Motors. Laurie promptly purchased four of the RTLs and gave this bus fleet number 64. The destination blind seems not to be suited to use on this bus. (Alan Mortimer)

Route number 178 was resurrected when single deck route 208A, operated by RF class vehicles, was replaced by RLH type buses on 13th May 1959. Operating on a weekday basis between Clapton Pond and Maryland Point at Stratford fourteen surplus vehicles were transferred to Dalston for the purpose, making that garage only the fourth Central Area one to operate the class. Here on 11th April RLH62, with route blind set for its return journey, pulls into the terminal stand at Clapton Pond. (John Gascoine)

Route 386 first received GS class buses in April 1954 some few months after the initial main batch had entered service. Still carrying an original 'Please Pay as you Enter' sticker in the quarter light together with the newest variety in its slipboard bracket, GS74 stands at St.Mary's Square as the shoppers in Hitchin market go about their business. The furthest destination of the 386 route from Hitchin was the Havers Lane Estate on the outskirts of Bishops Stortford but the next duty for this Hertford garage bus is a short 'swinger' just as far as Great Wymondley. In December the bus was to be delicensed and stored at Romford, London Road garage to await disposal. (Alan Mortimer)

These two views of RMF1254 were taken sometime between 29th October and 25th November while the bus was on loan to Liverpool Corporation Passenger Transport as shown by the sticker in the front bulkhead window. This was its first use in passenger service since being delivered to the Executive on 19th October. Various minor modifications were carried out to the vehicle in its early years of existence and these pictures show the original deep air intake and broken cream band between decks together with brake cooling ventilator grilles either side of the radiator. It was the only 1/7RM8 built and first appeared at the October Commercial Motor Show at Earls Court. It was destined never to be used in London in a normal revenue earning capacity. Several provincial loans and use within the capital on BEA Heathrow Airport services ended in October 1966 when it was delicensed to be sold the following month to Northern General. (both Alan Mortimer)

Thornton Heath Pond, looking more pedestrian friendly than nowadays, provides the resting place for RTL1630 on Route 159 before it heads for Kennington and then presumably its Camberwell garage home. The 'To & From Regent Street' slipboard carried on the bulkhead window is of course inappropriate for this particular journey. Having re-entered service from its March 1962 overhaul carrying a Park Royal body in place of its original Weymann example, the bus looks in resplendent condition. (W.R.Legg)

The life span of this Route 372 was only a little over four months commencing on 18th June and lasting until 23rd October. GS34 with route blind reading Avontar Road, Derwent Parade, Broxburn Drive admirably exhibits its localised nature, operating entirely within the confines of the Belhus Estate at South Ockendon. (Ron Wellings)

Catford garaged RT1218 carries a Weymann manufactured body in place of its original Saunders example. Due to the policy at this time whereby the Weymann and Park Royal bodies of the roof route number box variety were destined for early withdrawal, this RT would be disposed of in June of the following year. The bus carries a long lived example of the type of via point blind with five centrally placed names dating from the early nineteen fifties.

(Alan Mortimer)

Seen on 7th July at the London Road, Barking terminus of Route 169, Weymann bodied RT167, waits to depart for Barkingside High Street as duty BK266. The bus, which originally entered service at Croydon garage and was fitted then with a Park Royal body, was disposed of in December 1963 and sadly was left to deteriorate at Bird's Commercial Motors large yard at Stratford-upon-Avon until finally scrapped in April 1965. (John Gascoine)

Leyton garage was to be the final base for RT60, still carrying its original body number 311 and here, on 12th December entering Philip Lane at Tottenham High Cross approaching Tottenham garage. Its role as a learner bus commenced in June 1955 it having last been used in passenger service at New Cross. Before the end of 1963 it had been disposed of to George Cohen and scrapped, the end of a long career which stretched from January 1940 when the completed bus emerged from Chiswick works. (John Gascoine)

A nice touch is provided by Harrow Weald garage on RT2932 fitted with a Weymann RT3 body, number 1288. Eagle eyed viewers will note the proper use of the small vertical route number plate on the front bulkhead nearside pillar as the bus turns out of Bessborough Road at Harrow. The route number 158 which operated between Ruislip Lido and Watford Junction had a long history which stretched back to 1927 when the service was first introduced between South Harrow and Watford using K type buses from Edgware garage which were fitted with spragged gears to combat the hills at Bushey. The present day 258 route mimics the original version of the 158. (Alan Mortimer)

RT594 substitues for an RM on Route 269 and is seen crossing the junction at Wood Green Underground Station on its journey to Enfield. The conductor on the rear platform looks as though he has just been relieved and is ready to leap off at Wood Green garage half way up Jolly Butchers Hill ahead clutching his machine box. The RM following and the one making off in the opposite direction are engaged on Route 141. Not so long ago all the buses in this picture would have been trolleybuses and the Wood Green air would have been that much cleaner. (Alan Mortimer)

RT3910 is seen at the West Croydon Station terminus prior to departing for a short journey as far as Blackheath, Royal Standard in this sunless summer view. A number of interesting advertisements can be seen in the picture including Southern Electric's 'You're so near the West End by train' which features an old fashioned ticket barrier gate and a ticket collector apparently situated at Piccadilly Circus! There are free gifts galore to be had from Green Shield stamps - who remembers that short lived phenomenon? Finally various types of beverage adorn the hoardings and the bus. (Ron Wellings)

Enfield based RT3313 departs from Potters Bar garage on the Sunday only Route 242A to Upshire. The current body fitted was that which entered service as RT809 and as a consequence this fine looking bus was sold in December 1964, eventually to be operated by Blackford who traded as Isleworth Coaches but it only lasted until scrapped in 1968. (Ron Wellings)

RTW483 is seen on 25th April having re-entered service after its February overhaul from Battersea garage previously being in residence at Chalk Farm. This means that the 31 route jointly worked by these garages would not have been unfamiliar territory. The location is Kensington Church Street and included in this particular view an electric milk float of United Dairies is parked beside the kerb. Many of these vehicles seem to have incredibly long lives but this model, which appears to be one of the three wheeled variety steered with a sort of handlebar, is not one you see nowadays. (Tom Smith)

Leaving Garston garage to take up duties on Route 346A, Weymann bodied RT1042 looks cold and uninviting with all its windows closed in this picture taken sometime in January. The children, dressed against the elements, take no notice of the photographer or bus, busily occupied with other distractions. Having completed just over thirteen years of service as a Country Area vehicle, the bus has only just over two year's further service to complete before disposal. (A.B.Cross)

Parked in the St.Albans garage forecourt which was used as the terminus for several bus routes and short journeys on Green Line services, RF139 looks cold and uninviting. The skyline is unchanged to this day and once a year, usually in more pleasant weather conditions, a similar scene can be witnessed when the 'Save St.Albans Bus Garage' movement hold their annual rally on the same piece of ground hallowed to transport enthusiasts. (Alan Mortimer)

RT1309 stands within the Willesden garage yard adjoining Pound Lane. Although usurped from this northern terminus during the week by Route 176, Route 1 still journeyed between its more traditional termini of Willesden and Lewisham on Sundays. Since March this bus, originally fitted with a Saunders RT3/3 body, has carried this Park Royal RT8/2 example numbered 8466 and being of the ultimate style. (Ron Wellings)

New Saturday and Sunday route 278A was introduced on Saturday 6th January. On the previous Wednesday Route 278 had been revised to operate via Leytonstone Road and Forest Lane instead of Cann Hall Road and Dames Road. This was the first time Forest Lane, which parallels the railway track between Maryland and Forest Gate stations had received a bus route. On Saturday and Sunday Route 278A was introduced running from Stratford up to Maryland Station and then via the parent route. The Victoria & Albert Docks destination is qualified by 'via Balaam Street' to differentiate it from those routes which went 'via Greengate'. RM201 awaits departure from Stratford Broadway as duty WH88. (Ron Wellings)

RTL1545 negotiates Shepherds Bush Green at the start of its run in to Battersea Garage on 14th April on Route 49. This route through west and south London is one of the longer lasting examples dating back to 1912 and at various times it has reached Camden Town, Ealing Broadway, Wembley Stadium, Willesden Junction, Thornton Heath, Crystal Palace and Lewisham. The core section however between Kensington and Clapham Junction has remained constant to this day. (Roger Partridge)

RTL601 received an overhaul in January re-entering service from Middle Row garage. Three months later it is seen as it journeys along Kensington Church Street on Route 28 bound for Wandsworth, Armoury Way on 25th April. Following in service on Route 52 is RTL1053 whose home garage is just a short distance from the terminus of Victoria Station to which the bus is heading. (Tom Smith)

The date is 26th May and at the Royal Wells bus station in Cheltenham another ex-London bus, in this instance operated by Pulham & Sons of Bourton-on-the-Water, lays over before departure to its home town and the Rissingtons. Acquired by its new owners in June 1958 it was fitted with platform doors before entering service. After a ten year life of operation with its new owners ex-RTL36 found its way to Hartwood Finance, a dealer and breaker of South Yorkshire. (Tony R.Packer)

Emerging from Butterwick at Hammersmith on 14th April, Hertford garaged RF95 is seen carrying GF71 duty plates as it journeys to Guildford. The conductor is standing in a most unhelpful position as his driver tries to check the converging nearside traffic in his mirror. The good loading is typical of this route and these single deck coaches would be replaced in August by new double deck RMCs although the frequency of the route was reduced from 20 to 30 minute intervals. This RF first entered service in January 1952 and was refurbished and modernised later on in its life with London Transport eventually being reduced to scrap by Booth, the dealer of Rotherham, in April 1975. (Roger Partridge)

RT328 is seen at twenty past three on 25th April as duty J13 while in use on Route 27 bound for Teddington Station outside the offices of the 'Kensington News'. In July the bus was disposed of to Bird's Commercial Motors with the Weymann built body, number 1755, it bears here. Seven years later after service with Gibson Bros. of Barlestone it was exported to France to join an ever increasing number of the class which have travelled the short sea crossing to the continent. An interesting front advertisement is carried on the bus with the Daily Express offering the chance to win a new Zodiac car plus £5 a week for life. In 1962 over twenty gallons of petrol could be purchased allowing many miles of travel in your prize. Unfortunately the same cannot be said for the equivalent amount nowadays. (Tom Smith)

On snowy 2nd January Saunders bodied RT1896 is working from West Green garage as it turns off Hampstead Road into the northern part of Gower Street in service on Route 29 to Victoria. This was the early manifestation of the Tottenham Court Road one-way system. This was the last day of operation of West Green garage, the original 'Admiral' premises in Willow Walk and the normal RTLs had already been swopped with West Ham's RTs in readiness for the reallocation to Wood Green on the next day. (Alan Mortimer)

Route 259 was indirectly affected by the closure of West Green garage in January and eight RMs which had previously worked the route from Wood Green plus one new one from store were transferred to Tottenham which was on the line of route. With only one spare vehicle it was necessary for occasional substitutions and in this particular instance RTW46 is working duty AR5 as it heads north, bereft of custom, at Tramway Avenue, Edmonton on the weekend extension to Waltham Cross. (Alan Mortimer)

Only Hendon and Sutton garages were involved with operating RT4410 for any length of time from its entry into service during December 1953 at the former to its present use here in 1962. It did however spend a few days at Enfield garage following its one and only overhaul in May 1957. It re-entered service with body number 1556 in place of its original example, numbered 4713, which had previously been mounted on the chassis of SRT59. In its present guise it is seen opposite the pond at Sutton Green with the 'Relief Snack Bar' in the background, an appropriate name for a cafe at this location as the relief crew are now ready to continue the journey to Epsom station. (Alan Mortimer)

This particular scene is more interesting than a first glance might reveal. RT4562 leaves Two Waters garage bound for the Maylands Avenue industrial area on Route 377 which at its fullest ran from Apsley Mills to Redbourn. The London Transport bullseye mounted on the flat roof of the administration block reminds one who the owners of the garage are while in the right corner the unmistakable sloping rear of a Jowett Javelin car evokes memories of individually designed makes.
(Alan B.Cross)

RT4822 in company with RTL367 stand at the head of two lines of buses at Hounslow garage in the late summer. The RT carries interesting route blind for the London Transport service which operated between the various Bath Road car parks at London Airport Central and the terminal buildings. The RTL is employed on staff bus duties and has been since October 1959 following a year in unlicenced, unwanted storage. (Douglas F. Parker)

APPENDIX I

London Transport Central and Country Area Bus Garages

A	Sutton	K	Kingston
AB	Twickenham	L	Loughton
AC	Willesden	LH*	Leatherhead
AD	Palmers Green	LS*	Luton
AE	Hendon	M	Mortlake
AF	Chelverton Road, Putney	MA*	Amersham
AK	Streatham	MH	Muswell Hill
AL	Merton	N	Norwood
AM	Plumstead	NB	Norbiton
AP	Seven Kings	NF*	Northfleet
AR	Tottenham	NS	North Street, Romford
AV	Hounslow	NX	New Cross
AW	Abbey Wood	ON	Alperton
B	Battersea	PB	Potters Bar
BK	Barking	PM	Peckham
BN	Brixton	PR	Poplar
BW	Bow	Q	Camberwell
BX	Bexleyheath	R	Riverside
CF	Chalk Farm	RD	Hornchurch
CM*	Chelsham	RE*	London Road, Romford
CN	Carshalton	RG*	Reigate
CS	Chiswick (non-operational)	RL	Rye Lane
CT	Clapton	S	Shepherds Bush
CY*	Crawley	SA*	St.Albans
D	Dalston	SF	Stamford Hill
DG*	Dunton Green	SJ*	Swanley Junction
DS*	Dorking	SP	Sidcup
DT*	Dartford	ST*	Staines
E	Enfield	SV*	Stevenage
ED	Elmers End	SW	Stockwell
EG*	East Grinstead	T	Leyton
EM	Edmonton	TB	Bromley
EP*	Epping	TC	Croydon
EW	Edgware	TG*	Tring
FY	Finchley	TH	Thornton Heath
GD*	Godstone	TL	Catford
GF*	Guildford	TW*	Tunbridge Wells
GM	Gillingham Street, Victoria	U	Upton Park
GR*	Garston	UX	Uxbridge
GY*	Grays	V	Turnham Green
H	Hackney	W	Cricklewood
HB	Hammersmith (BEA Coaches)	WD	Wandsworth
HD	Harrow Weald	WG	West Green
HE*	High Wycombe	WH	West Ham
HF*	Hatfield	WL	Walworth
HG*	Hertford	WN	Wood Green
HH*	Two Waters, Hemel Hempstead	WR*	Windsor
HL	Hanwell	WW	Walthamstow
HT	Highgate	WY*	Addlestone
HW	Southall	X	Middle Row
J	Holloway	-	Aldenham (non-operational)

* indicates a Country Area garage.

This is a list of all operational garages together with the two main non-operational sites for bus maintenance as at 1st January 1962.

Two garages were brought into operation during the year, both having been converted from trolleybus depots:

FW   Fulwell commenced motor bus operation on 9th May
SE   Stonebridge Park commenced motor bus operation on 3rd January.

One garage closed during the year and that was West Green (WG). Its allocation of 66 RTL class buses being transferred to West Ham (WH), which took 64 and Tottenham (AR) which had the other two. These RTLs were swopped with RTs many of which operated for a day or so from West Green before being transferred on closure to Wood Green (WN) who took over duties on Routes 29, 144, 217, 231 and 233. Route 29A went to Palmers Green (AD) while the small allocation on Route 171 went to Tottenham (AR).

Outside the scope of this series of books but for the sake of completeness, trolleybus depots Colindale (CE) and Isleworth (IH) were closed.

RTL8 was disposed of to Bird's Commercial Motors in August 1958, subsequently being purchased by S. Eynon of Trimsaran, Carmarthenshire the following month. It is now fitted with body number 6612 first carried by RTL1361 and some four years younger than the 1948 built chassis. Lengthwise advertising carried on the bus announces that the 'Dragon Stores' of Thomas Street, Llanelly, delivered free your beers, wines and spirits, while one of the latest films to reach the immediate locality is "High Society" soon to be showing at the Odeon Cinema. (Tony R.Packer)

APPENDIX II

Thanks are extended to the following correspondents for providing helpful comments and information to update or correct earlier titles in this series of books. They are Allan T.Condie, Keith Gregory, Ken D.Jubb and Michael Lockyer.

1947 BOOK

Page 16   The lower picture is of RT16, not 15 as the caption states. Therefore body details need amending to read that this bus did not keep its original body, receiving number 291, ex-RT30, in September 1946. Its completion and entry into service are as captioned but it was disposed of to Bird's Commercial Motors in September 1960.

1956 BOOK

Page 20   The photograph of STL1158 should be credited to Brian Rackham whose surname I have spelt incorrectly as Rackman. This unfortunate spelling error also occurs on page 80 of the 1961 book with the photograph of STL1985. I proffer my sincere apologies.

Page 125   The lower picture of ex-D220 requires two comments which have been brought to the author's attention. Firstly quite a few of Ledgard's ex-D class buses were fitted with doors, mainly it is suspected to disguise the fact that there were no heaters fitted! Secondly, the radiator plate now carries the legend 'Samuel Ledgard' in place of the former 'London Transport'.

Page 134   The STs are pictured at Lawrence Hill depot just outside the Central Repair Works. Bristol Tramways had the buses on loan as it was not until 1956 that the title 'Bristol Omnibus Company Ltd.' came into use.

1961 BOOK

Page 37   RO699 (G151) is just turning off the Glasgow Road into the rear entrance of Perth depot.

Page 53   RO712 (G298) is seen crossing South Street on Scott Street travelling on the Moncrieff - Muirton service 113.

Page 70   RO696 (G66) was the only Guy Arab I to reach Alexanders and again is seen in Scott Street heading from Friarton to Muirton North on service 109.

Page 86   The registration number VD4437 once belonged to a Leyland TD4 with lowbridge body which was new to Central SMT in 1935 and which was withdrawn and sold in 1952 to Cooper, a showman of Glasgow. The bus shown here has been confirmed as being totally an ex-STD with unique LT pattern dumb iron covers. A case of identity swopping but the STD fleet number still remains a mystery at present.

Page 154   Ex-RT1479 is seen in Market Street, Cannock one of the town centre loading points prior to the opening of the bus station.